INSTANT BOATS

INSTANT BOATS

BY HAROLD H. PAYSON

INTERNATIONAL MARINE PUBLISHING COMPANY
CAMDEN, MAINE

Plans for the boats in this book, as well as additional designs, are available from:

Harold H. Payson
South Thomaston, ME 04858

Copyright © 1979
by International Marine Publishing Company
Library of Congress Catalog Card Number 78-64738
International Standard Book Number 0-87742-110-2
Typeset by A & B Typesetters, Inc., Concord, New Hampshire
Printed and bound by The Alpine Press, Inc., Stoughton, Massachusetts
Second printing, 1982

Published by International Marine Publishing Company
21 Elm Street, Camden, Maine 04843

To my father, Herman W. Payson, who could build a castle with nothing but an ax.

And to the memory of my father-in-law, Archie H. Rackliff, boatbuilder, fisherman, and friend, who offered encouragement, but not his boat molds, instead saying, "Go build your own boat."

Contents

Foreword

People who build boats because they like carpentry build better boats, and have less grief, than those who build because they want a boat they can't afford. The former are admirable and valuable, but I have more empathy with the latter. I used to build a boat every so often because I thought I ought to, but I grudged money for good tools and time to learn much skill. Once, when I was about ready to launch, a friendly bystander remarked, "If you back off 50 feet, that boat looks real good."

The trouble with the quick-and-dirty idea is that the dirty work is not apt to be quick. Dull tools make work slow as well as rough. Harold Payson has been working for years, tempting people who can't drive a nail straight to start learning to work quick-and-*clean*. It's rare for a man with so much skill to take an interest in such people, rarer still to write so vividly about them, rarest of all for the skilled man to keep his insight into the light of ignorance.

My plans that illustrate the book have been wrung out hard to dry up the mistakes. They've been corrected rather than redrawn to make sure no new mistakes crept in. In coping with them, the author was between the devil (a designer full of enthusiasm but with a limited grasp of the nature of the problems) and the deep sea (would-be amateur boatbuilders—as a class not the most sensible crew alive). Read on: he's equal to the occasion.

Philip C. Bolger

RESOLUTION, Gloucester

Acknowledgments

For the writing of this book, I owe thanks to many:

To Bill Prosser, who gave me a proper heading and kept me on course.

To my wife, Amy, for doing all the typing and cheering me on when only one page was a day's work. To my children Timothy and Lisa, who suffered silence instead of rock and roll.

Special thanks to Peter Spectre, former editor for International Marine Publishing, for taking personal interest in this book from start to finish and for always making me feel at home in his office.

To Brooks Townes, former assistant editor of *National Fisherman,* who knew what a job I had ahead of me but never told me until after the book was well along.

To Dennis Hansen and Lance Gunderson for sharing their boatbuilding experiences.

To Karin Knudsen for her courage and determination in building the Teal from start to finish.

To the builders in the past who have taken the trouble to write me (some good—some not so good); for all, I am grateful.

To future builders—just for comparison of what is easy to what isn't—I can truthfully say that it was far easier for me to build the boats than it was to write about how to build them.

INSTANT BOATS

1

Introduction

This book is dedicated to the proposition that building a boat, while difficult, can be made reasonably easy. Take note of that word *reasonably*. Miracles are scarce in the boatbuilding business, and there is no royal road to learning. You can encounter a considerable amount of grief in building the simplest type of craft. This is because boatbuilding is primarily an attempt to produce a nicely curved, three-dimensional shape out of two-dimensional materials, which is guaranteed to produce some problems in making all those flat pieces of wood come together gracefully. All boatbuilders must therefore get involved with beveling, and bending, and working with angles and curves.

How to build Instant Boats—a concept I will describe shortly—is the subject of this book. It's always rewarding to find that what one hoped would work really did end up working. When Steve Saft of the *National Fisherman* staff said at the launching of the first 12-foot Teal, "I don't have any mechanical skills at all, but I really think even I could build that one," it was the sort of reaction designer Phil Bolger and I were looking for.

The Instant Boat idea wasn't a speculative concept dreamed up out of a blue sky. I had been selling boat plans for years, and I had been getting too many letters from customers saying they couldn't build a boat from them. When I'd ask, "Did you loft it full size first?" the reply I got would be, "What's lofting?"

Other would-be builders would ask me: "Do you think I can build a boat?" A good question, I always thought, but how could I answer it when I didn't have the least idea of the prospective builder's skills?

1

Determination is evident in the expression of Eldon Collamore, a Bremen, Maine, boatbuilder. This photograph, originally published in the National Fisherman *in 1966, has graced the author's boatshop walls since then to provide inspiration for his many projects. (Photo by E.L. Boutilier)*

Designing not being one of my talents, I turned to Phil Bolger to see what he could come up with. I supposed that, like other designers, he had had his share of designs that never were built and would be familiar with the problem of the first-time builder. He wrote back saying he would do it, but there would be just one catch to it. I'd have to build all of the boats he designed first to make sure they would go together as designed and to check the plans for any inaccuracies. He didn't want me sending out plans that didn't work.

I thought this reasonable enough, reflecting on some of my own moments out on Penobscot Bay when I was lobstering, and would have dearly loved to have my boat designer aboard to see firsthand what he had created.

As usual, Phil came through. His Instant Boat designs drastically simplified the building process and slashed the time required. They also carried simplicity a step beyond my idea, by making all but the kayak possible to be built using only 4 x 8 plywood sheets and 2 x 4s commonly found at the local lumberyard.

Some schools have bought boat plans for their woodworking departments in recent years, responding to the renewed interest in wooden boatbuilding. (That's what I would have liked to have done in school, but I ended up making a trinket box and a table lamp instead.) I think these schools could take a leaf from the Instant Boat book. I've yet to hear a teacher report that a boat had been finished in school. When I heard from a teacher at Queens College in New York that he and his students were planning to build a Cape Ann dory, I warned him that a "simple" lapstrake dory isn't as easy as it looks. I didn't for one second believe they would take my advice and choose something easier.

Of course they didn't, and later I received a letter saying: "You were quite right about the difficulty of building the dory. Our students did their homework, and read all available material on layout, etc., but the term ended before the construction got underway."

I think this is typical of a lot of schools—too much theory with nothing to show for it. With no boat produced to look at, both theory and desire disappear into thin air, and the potential builders are effectively turned off from ever making anything.

On the other hand, the Instant Boats have eliminated lofting and building jigs, and have cut down the time element, so that it is possible for you to get out on the water in your own boat and be sailing while you're contemplating going on to greater things. Guess I'm prejudiced, but I think sailing in even one of these simple craft is a helluva lot better than sitting on the bank on a warm summer's day with a head full of theory.

But you do not wholly escape *all* problems, even in building an Instant Boat. If that could be done, you would probably end up with a hull that would look as though it were made from an excellent design for something to mix cement in (I've done that, too, in my long-gone youthful days). You want a boat that looks like a boat—and, incidentally, the more a boat looks like a boat, the more likely it is that it will behave like a boat when it meets the water.

Instant Boats do pare down the problems to a minimum. If you have average skills with tools and can saw along a penciled line, your Instant Boat will take shape in a surprisingly short time. Builders with no more than a modest amount of skill have built some Instant Boats in one 40-hour workweek. One woman, whose pictures appear later on, started from ground zero, and even though she had to learn to use tools before she could learn to build boats, she completed her 12-foot sailboat in just 90 working hours.

INSTANT BOATS

When I say building Instant Boats is "reasonably easy," note that the first word of the phrase contains the word *reason*. You must exercise your grey cells, or use plain common sense, when you are working to construct a good-looking and functional shape that will get the most out of wind and wave. You cannot just whomp her together, get in, and sail away. You can never cheat on your boat; you have to give her your full attention and all the benefit of whatever level of çommon sense you are blessed with. This includes using the right tools for the job, and keeping those tools in good functioning order. You won't need a lot of tools, but they must be the right ones. Planes, saws, and chisels must be kept sharp; paint brushes must be kept clean rather than matted with goo; and the hammerhead face must be maintained in good condition. All this will be discussed in later chapters.

Materials, too, deserve respect. You cannot begin with bargain-basement wood and expect to end up with a sound hull. You must put a just value on every component that goes into your boat, whether it's one of hundreds of nails, or a strip of fiberglass tape, or the glue that helps bond any one of a dozen joints. They're all part of your boat, and they will make themselves known by good performance or embarrassing failure sooner or later after launching day.

About mistakes: everybody makes them, and so will you. On this subject I want to give a nod to the late Howard I. Chapelle, who served the boatbuilding and design world through many fine books and through his work as a marine historian. I never had the good fortune to meet Mr. Chapelle, but I am convinced by one remark in his classic work *Boatbuilding* (W.W. Norton, N.Y.) that he was acquainted firsthand with the actual construction of boats in a not-too-professional one-man shop. That single observation proves that he had been there, alone with a few tools and some stubborn pieces of wood and metal that were being coaxed into a serviceable watercraft. I am referring to his dictum that every boatbuilding shop should include a piece of furniture called the Moaning Chair, which is to be used as an alternative to hanging yourself in a closet or blowing your brains out in the backyard after you have discovered that you have made the bonehead mistake of all time, or so it seems, and have ended up with a wretched mess of wood and fastenings beyond redemption. That is the time, said Chapelle, when the boatbuilder should slump down in his Moaning Chair and moan. He further insists that he should remain in it until the period of moaning is over, and that when he emerges he should walk wide of his fledgling craft, not even laying a finger on it. Instead, he should go off and look at the scenery or occupy himself with some other harmless diversion until sanity returns. Only then can he go back and assess the real damage (which, in my experience, has always been less than I thought) and determine how he can get himself out of the hole he has dug.

The Instant Boat concept drastically cuts down on the frequency of use of the Moaning Chair. The boats designed for this type of building are as simple as can be—no lofting or jig required—not through crudity but through the exercise of the expertise and ingenuity of Phil Bolger. The end result will be graceful, satisfying, and functionally successful.

Just keep the phrase *reasonably easy* in the forefront of your mind, and don't neglect the use of reason. Most important of all, *get started*! The sooner you begin, the closer you will be to the proud day when you launch, man, and sail away a boat you made with your own hands. After many years of experience, I can testify that life holds very, very few more satisfying moments.

For those of you who, after reading this book, still find yourselves a little timid or doubtful of your practical capabilities, there are always kit boats available from other sources. But before going that route, I encourage you to bite the bullet and go ahead with an Instant Boat, for building a boat, or anything else, from scratch is in the end a good booster shot for morale.

Instant Boats have been designed with the belief that there are brave tyros out there who can face up to a mistake, pick themselves up, and keep going to the finish. Even the pro will enjoy building one as a refreshing interlude from wrestling with more complex types. As for the novice, he will find that these little boats will offer a modest challenge that, when overcome, will leave him with a substantially greater measure of self-respect.

The Kayak, all 12 feet of her, powered by the author's son Neil.

Above: *The Teal, a 12-foot stretched punt. (Photo by Steve Saft)*

Below: *The Folding Schooner, 31 feet, with designer Phil Bolger aboard.*

The Elegant Punt, seven feet nine inches. (Photo by Stan Walsh)

The Surf, a 15-foot six-inch crab skiff that is a favorite of the author's. (Photo by Stan Walsh)

The Zephyr, 20 feet nine inches.

2

The Good of Wood

When you build your Instant Boat, obviously it will be made of wood. Nevertheless, I want to ramble on about wood a little, partly because you should be fully aware of just how lucky you are that you will end up with a wooden craft and partly because I have had a long-standing love affair with the stuff. For me, at least, the joy of working with wood amounts to a never-ending infatuation. One of the many reasons is that it has its own personality. It also poses a challenge. Yet to the first-time builder it can be an unforgiving teacher. A piece of wood that was intended to be sawed out straight as a die—say, for a small keel for an outboard boat—and mysteriously emerges with a definite and wholly unwelcome curve, can cause the novice to throw up his arms in despair. This very contrariness of wood, however, is one of the things that makes working with it an interesting and certainly never-boring process.

The building of Instant Boats avoids all the trickier quirks of wood, but it can be helpful to understand a little more of the nature of the beast than will be actually required to put your boat together. And it gives me a chance to shoot the breeze a little.

When I was a novice boatbuilder, I had a golden opportunity to observe a pro who knew exactly what would happen when wood runs up against a saw blade. I had just begun building boats in earnest when I found I needed a straight oak keel measuring two inches by two and a half inches by fourteen feet, and had no saw capable of handling such a timber. So I went to the Makinen Brothers' boatyard in South Thomaston, Maine. Now, the uninformed visitor who dropped in on Amos and Bill's shop looking for a place to have a boat built would very likely take one quick look around and get the hell out as fast as possible. The shop's dirt floor and ramshackle-looking machinery, plus a general impression of just plain litter, would not give the casual stranger any evidence of the dozens and dozens of smart, seaworthy hulls that had been constructed there. His impressions would not be helped, either, by the general attitude of the brothers, who were expert at assuming a *haven't done a damn thing all day, and don't plan to either* kind of look.

I was not fooled by the Makinens or their shop, because I was familiar with the able boats they turned out. But even for me—and I was a frequent visitor, sneaking in quietly to learn some of the fine points of the trade—it was hard to surprise them actually at work. For one thing, they had an exasperating habit of dropping whatever it was they were doing to gam with you. I tried to drop in when they were in the middle of something they couldn't just walk away from—for example, setting up the stations for one of their hulls—but never succeeded. Everything always seemed to have been done already, and I began to think that erecting the molds that gave their product their sweet (sorry, there isn't any other word) shape was something the Makinens did in the middle of the night with drawn blinds. Every time I went there, the molds would be all set up with ribbands in place, ready for planking.

On this particular day, even *my* faith was shaken for a little while. When I asked Amos if he could get me a keel of the dimensions I needed, as straight as humanly possible, he unclasped his hands from behind his back and gave me a "Guess so." With that we went out to a huge, haphazard pile of live-edge oak. (Planks with live edges have yet to be squared off; their edges still conform to the shape of the tree.) The Makinens' homemade saw rig was nearby, outdoors and uncovered. Like their thickness planer, the saw was powered with a converted car engine and transmission. Neither one had a radiator, so once they got either of them started—usually with an old battery with seemingly only one last spark left in it—they worked at flank speed to get done what cutting or planing needed doing before the old engine got overheated.

Amos picked out a piece and began the standard operating procedure for starting the engine. As usual, it did not start the first time. It had no choke, so Amos cupped his hand over the carburetor to give her a gulp of gas, hit the starter button, and again—nothing. So he reached in his pocket, produced a nail, and drove it between the battery terminal and the cable connector. This time, after the cupped-hand choke routine, when he pushed the button, she went.

While the engine was warming up to the point where he knew she wouldn't stall, Amos dug out a thin batten and struck a graceful curve on the selected piece of oak. I couldn't believe what I was seeing—I had told him I wanted my piece straight, and there he was putting a deliberate bend in his cutting line! Knowing that boatbuilders are temperamental people, even though it was obvious that he hadn't heard me right, I held back from tugging at Amos's sleeve and shouting above the roar of the old motor that he was going about it all wrong. Better to wait and take the blame for not telling him what I wanted in just the right way, I thought, than invite the wrath of a man who had built as many good boats as he had without any help from me. Besides, no doubt I would have occasion to come back for something, sometime, and I did not want to find myself unwelcome. So I struggled to keep my mouth shut, for once.

And just as well I did. For when the stick came clear of the saw, it was as straight and true as anyone could wish. I remember thinking, as I took the piece of wood and paid what Amos asked for it (not much, either), that any man who can know in advance just how much a piece of oak will straighten out when the inner stress is released after it has been run through the saw deserves to sit on the right hand of God, or at least win the jackpot prize in the State Lottery. For me it was an on-the-spot lesson that trees grow with built-in dynamics—something Amos obviously already knew all about, and could judge and take advantage of, just by looking at the grain.

The point of this story, for the Instant Boat builder or anyone else, is that fancy equipment isn't needed for quality work (and won't guarantee it anyway). It ain't what you do it with, it's just how you do it. Another lesson is that live-edge timber is best for boat work, because the natural curve of the tree itself can be utilized to suit individual bending requirements, with a minimum of edge-setting or forcing planking into position, something to avoid whenever possible.

While we're on planking (which will not concern you as you build your Instant Boat, but may someday if you decide to go in for other boatbuilding techniques), I want to comment that any wood I have ever used, other than plywood, has a tendency to cup or curl after it has reached a certain degree of dryness. Planking is much easier if you take note of the direction of the curl and lay the concave side of the plank against the frames, especially at the turn of the bilge, where the planks must be hollowed a little with a gouge plane. Nature has already done some of the hollowing for you if you do it this way, and works against you if you don't. But be careful when determining which way the plank has cupped. Inspection of the annular growth rings in the end of a plank would seem to indicate that it will cup in the same direction as the rings. Not so; in fact, it will cup in exactly the opposite direction. A board sawed through its whole length with the heart nearly dead center in the board will cup only very slightly, if at all.

There is another interesting facet to wood when it is used in boatbuilding. This is the apparent change of shape that takes place when a piece of it is fastened where it belongs. You see this in planking, for example, when strakes with some pretty peculiar curves and tapers appear uniform and horizontal when they have been wrapped around the molds or forms. Sometimes they take on a flavor of the fantastic. This can be most extreme in the garboard strake—next to the keel—in a round-bottomed hull of some complexity.

I remember an incident that took place in one of the oldest and most highly respected shipyards on the coast of Maine, one noted for many famous vessels and for high standards of yacht finish. Because of a large Navy contract, this yard was forced to expand its experienced cadre of old-line craftsmen with a heavy influx of warm bodies to work under their supervision. At the time, this yard was also building a sizable yawl as a contender for Bermuda Race honors, and for this proud craft the most experienced master builder in the outfit took on as his personal project the lofting, lining off, and shaping of the two garboards, port and starboard. When completed, these perfectly matched, intricately shaped pieces of near-priceless mahogany looked to the unpracticed eye like nothing on earth practical or useful, real or imagined. At least they appeared so to one pair of unpracticed eyes whose owner had been told to saw up some scrap for firewood. That's right. And when the fate of the two garboards was reported to the master builder, he all but wept. He also all but soared through the shop roof, and the innocent vandal had to keep out of his sight for some weeks to avoid becoming a victim of manslaughter.

A little bit far-out in a discussion of building Instant Boats? Not really. This peculiarity of flat pieces of wood to transform themselves when bent works both ways. The six boats from which you are about to make a choice use this principle to work in your favor. When you cut the sides of your Teal or Zephyr, for example, you will be dealing with straight, penciled lines, and your only problem will be to avoid wandering off them. You then fasten them together, bending them in the process, and *presto!*—you will have built a nicely curved and gracefully sheered hull. All cut, mind you, on the straight.

WOOD LASTS, AND LASTS, AND LASTS

The first crude boat ever launched was doubtless made of wood. In modern times, all kinds of materials have been sent to sea. In addition to the obvious ones, there is an English sailboat whose hull, mast, and spars were all made of pages from the *London Times*—tightly rolled up and lavishly glued, of course, and laid up in many layers for her outer skin, the whole thing well varnished. Some day, some adventurous soul will build a craft of shredded wheat biscuits and caulk it with peanut butter.

Right now there are at least a dozen wooden vessels still afloat after more than a hundred years. The Scandinavian Viking *Gokstad* ship was found in an amazing state of preservation after being buried for nearly a thousand years, and the Swedish Royal man-of-war *Vasa* was recently refloated from the bottom of the sea, several centuries after she sank. I don't blame fiberglass craft and ferrocement hulls for not having racked up comparable tests of time—they haven't had the opportunity. But wood has, and has passed the test.

"Where are all the fish?" A lobsterboat that's seen better days. (Photo by Brooks Townes)

From my own experience, I can vouch for two examples of the durability of wooden craft. One of them was a planked-up outboard lobsterboat of my own. During a trip by trailer she became airborne, sailed past my truck, and slammed into a stone wall at the same speed I was driving. The result is shown above. Can you wonder that the general advice of well-wishers was unanimous, "burn her"? Well, we didn't. We reconstructed her—and, with the exception of one minor fragment, we were able to use all the original planking. Take a look at the "after" picture.

On page 17 is another set of before-and-after photos. This one was an old and quite yachty power launch. It's an open question when she was built, but it was certainly before the year 1900. She was more or less deeded to me by her last previous owner, on condition that I fix her up. She had just plain been neglected. When I say neglected, it was by no means the fault of the previous owner, Phil Ware of Spruce Head Island, Maine, now in his nineties. He had taken excellent care of her, and had stored her in an old building for a number of years with the intention of fixing her up and painting her himself. He had gone so far as to remove all the old paint down to the bare wood, strip the hardware, and take everything off that would be hard to paint around. He had even taken care to record the original location of all the pieces of ceiling that

14

The lobsterboat opposite, after the shape has been restored with a Spanish windlass, the fiberglass has been peeled back, a new plank has been put in, and all the planks have been eased into the stem rabbet.

Several layers of new fiberglass have been applied with polyester resin.

The renewed boat, after the bow has been primed. It's ready for water except for the finish coat.

he removed, and had carefully kept all the screws that he removed, also. What raised havoc with the planking was bringing her to my shop to wait for repairs. There was no place inside to store her. A year rightside-up with no covering didn't help her any, and another upside-down with the sun beating on her made matters worse—her planks became checked and cupped.

As bad as the problems looked, the launch could still have been made reasonably tight as long as she was left in the water, but my patience has long gone for dealing with leaky boats, so I decided to cover her with a couple of layers of fiberglass cloth, guaranteeing freedom from any future worry of watertightness. In this case, not one stick of new wood had to be added. It was a matter of scrape, sand, polish, recaulk, repaint, and revarnish. Some of the metalwork was in the worst shape, but with the volunteered services of my friend John Taylor of South Thomaston, Maine, what could be polished bright was, and what could not was turned out new on a lathe. The propeller and her one-lung gasoline engine took the most refurbishing. When we were finished, the owner inspected her and declared her better than new—or, at least, when new to him. She passed her sea trials with flying colors.

Even for a professional, boatbuilding oftentimes becomes a matter of making do with what's at hand. Take, for instance, the problem of dealing with the idiosyncrasies of wood. I am not fortunate enough to work in a consistently warm climate. If I did, I could put to work the pull of the sun and the moisture in the ground to straighten some naturally cussed piece of wood long enough to get glue and fastenings to hold for assembly. In our brief periods of "tropical" weather in Maine, I do so by putting down the concave side of the board out of doors. The moisture from the ground will swell the underside and cause it to flatten, while the sun is shrinking the top side. With both sun and moisture working together, sometimes it's only a matter of minutes before the board is as straight as could be.

But in the winter it's up to the old woodstove in the shop to do the job. My first acquaintance with this antique goes back to my childhood—it was the sole thermal energy source for the one-room schoolhouse I attended through the eighth grade and had been there for years before I went to school. It's probably approaching its first centennial. After the school was converted to oil heat, the stove saw service in every kind of weather as a garbage burner until it and the schoolhouse were both abandoned. I hauled it home for my then-new shop. With a few straps and bolts to hold the rig together, it looks as if it will last as long as I'll ever need it. Granted, the old stove is no match for nature's elements in pulling a board straight—it's much slower. But who cares? I'm punching no time clock.

We were on the subject of the strength and durability of wood. If we want to be fancy, we can talk in terms of its tensile strength and its compression strength. Let's leave it that it's tough and flexible. You can drag a wooden bottom over some pretty rough sea floor, pounding as you go at that, and all

BEFORE: A long-neglected power launch built before 1900.

AFTER: The resurrected power launch, following scraping, sanding, polishing, caulking, fiberglassing, painting, and varnishing.

you might have is a few scratches and maybe a gouge or two to fill in come haul-out time. Sizable wooden vessels with a lot more weight than your Instant Boat, and carrying a good deal of inside ballast, have been through that experience and required little more than a recaulking job between a few strakes.

In building your Instant Boat, you will be working with plywood, which has one disadvantage: it will not bend in two different directions at the same time. The design of a boat meant to be built in plywood has to be drawn with this firmly in mind. This characteristic of plywood is taken into consideration in the plans Phil Bolger has provided for you, and I have put each boat to the test by actually building the prototype.

Plywood's resistance to two-directional twisting springs from one of its virtues—that it does not have one consistent grain of wood but rather is layered up of opposing grains. This gives plywood its unique strength and is a blessing.

Plywood is probably the best choice for the first-time builder, for these reasons: economy, availability, longevity, weight, and one-piece construction for tightness and speed of building.

Years ago, when plywood was first used in boatbuilding, I was one of the many who said they would never use it. Having seen plenty of leaky and chewed-up plywood boats around, I felt that their chines and bottom planking were no match for Maine's tough, rock-filled waters. What used to bother me about plywood was that the rest of the boat would look like new, but the edge grain of the chines and other exposed areas would be all broken up. After a few scrapings and poundings, the boat would leak and look past its time. That was before the age of fiberglass. Since then, the use of fiberglass as a reinforcement has changed the whole picture. The splintered, leaky plywood hull became one of absolute tightness and long life, adequately protected along the vulnerable areas that were once so easily damaged.

With ever-changing prices, it's pointless to compare costs of building small boats today, so we will just take a look at plywood grades and their relative prices in a general sense. Marine grade is the best and is, of course, the most expensive. Exterior grade for the last two years, and at the time of writing, is so poor that it is not worth lugging home. For instance ⅜-inch marine grade has five plies, a fact that pretty well eliminates the chances of voids causing trouble. The ⅜-inch exterior stuff is another matter. It has three plies with a center core about ¼-inch thick; sometimes there are voids running the whole width of the sheet. That's bad enough for the strength factor, but what is worse than that is that the plywood companies cover over the edge voids of plywood with a substance about the color of peanut butter. This matches the color of the wood so well that, even on close inspection, the voids can go undetected until the plywood is brought home and sawed into, or until the hammerhead goes through the sheet.

Outright deception is what it is, and it has only been practiced in the past few years. It used to be that exterior grade was plenty good enough for boatbuilding. Now there seem to be two choices: either marine grade or, strangely enough, the cheapest grade of plywood available, called shop grade. Shop grade is plywood that has corners nicked and other uglies in it. It has a good core and one good face; the other side is knotty. The glue used in shop grade is marine glue, which will not allow delamination, but the best part of the deal is the price—about one-fourth the price of marine grade. The outside knots are not really a problem because they are readily seen and lend themselves to easy patching. The surfaces aren't sanded as well as marine grade, but I think that the price makes this of little concern. I have seen some boats built of shop grade that were given a coat of epoxy, and as far as I can see, they are as durable as the marine-grade plywood. It seems as though shop grade is well worth looking into.

When developing the Instant Boat concept, Phil Bolger showed his usual good judgment and realized that it made sense to design a fleet of small boats using materials that could be had at one stop at the nearest lumber company. That meant specifying 8-foot plywood sheets and 2 x 4s for framing. Because of heavy demand, these are always in stock and always competitive in price, which guarantees a long-time supply. An Instant Boat can always be in the reach of almost any would-be boatbuilder.

So there you have it. The materials are at hand and are not prohibitively costly. The plans are available, and they have been proven in the shop and on the water. If you do not have every tool you could possibly want, so what? Chances are you will need to invest in only one or two at most (extensive discussion of tools comes later). If you don't have a Skilsaw, you can take your plywood sheets to a shop where the long, straight cuts can be done for you. The rest can be done with a handsaw (and so could the long cuts, for that matter—the activity might be healthier and more fun than jogging).

3

Beginner's Luck (Mostly Bad)

As a one-time amateur boatbuilder myself, I can speak with authority on the beginner's problems. My first boat looked like a cement-mixing box. However, the process of building it had two of the prime essentials: a start and a finish, with a lot of determination in between. I was thirteen. But I did start it and I did finish it, and those are two very important things about building a boat. (My father, Herman W. Payson, *really* finished it, when—fearing for my safety, I suppose—he took an ax and reduced it to splinters.)

Why does the beginner have trouble producing *anything*?

In my experience there are three types of would-be builders who go aground in the successful production of a boat. The first is the type who knows better than the designer. He can't stand to follow directions. He is the first to complain that the boat couldn't possibly be built from the inadequate plans with which he has been burdened. His complaining letter to the seller of the plans states that the designer's measurements are all screwed up and no one could possibly build a boat from them. This falls a little flat on my ears, especially when I know that at least a hundred boats have already been built from those plans.

Next comes the tinkerer, or modifier. He starts with the plans for a pretty little sailboat and studies them thoroughly. He hasn't had the experience of being in a number of different boats under varying sea conditions, but he's smart. He has read a lot—perhaps he has worked with computers and is a confirmed student of tank tests. With all the bravery of a matador in the bull ring, he lops six inches off the rudder (or just as likely adds it on). He also decides the mast is too long or too short, or the boat's scantlings are too light or too heavy. He builds something he calls his boat, tries her out, and then sits down to write me a letter saying she has excessive weather helm or lee helm and asking what the matter can be.

Here's an extreme example—a European builder who bought a stock plan of a 22-foot sailing dory with a 600-pound ballasted keel, with a small cuddy forward (this is not an Instant Boat, but the example still holds). He wrote that he had built her exactly to plan and sent a picture to prove it. Well, the hull lines were all right, *but*—there was no mast, there was no keel. However, he had not stinted. He put power in her, and tacked on a spacious full-headroom pilothouse aft and a trunk cabin forward. His letter said: "After the first trial, it was found the boat is unstable without ballast. Could you inform me how many kilograms I have to drive in the bilge?" My stock reply seemed to fit the situation: "I don't know. I'm not a designer; I just build them."

Type number three is quite harmless. He is The Perfectionist, and he simply takes a long time getting anything at all done, for fear of making a mistake. He is the one who finds a quick place (an unfair curve) in his batten after bending it precisely along the naval architect's measurements or offsets. The shock of finding out that the designer has made a mismeasurement, and is thus not really some kind of god, throws him into a dither, so he delays proceeding with building until he can learn to cope with other people's minor mistakes.

You don't believe it? Consider the novice builder who bought a piece of wood from me to make a dory stem. He was a machine designer who was accustomed to working with extremely close tolerances, say, to the thousandth of a cat's whisker. Several months later I asked him how it came out. It seems he hadn't got up the courage to make a single cut in it. It was safely tucked away under his bed.

STOP, LOOK—AND LOOK AGAIN

You can make mistakes without completely belonging to any of these three categories; I've proved it myself. I never did learn the trade by working in a shop or with another builder. So what mistakes I made were paid for out of hide and pocket. One thing I'm sure of is that mistakes made and paid for that way are less likely to be repeated.

Take the case of the ruined plank. One of the easiest and most exasperating of all mistakes is a mismeasurement on a long plank that has been fitted for a round-bottom hull. This can happen on a straight piece for an Instant Boat; don't think it can't. In this case I had spent hours of time and many ergs of energy on shaping this particular plank—getting the taper and the bevels just right, and hollowing its inner side to fit the turn of the bilge. The rule I used wasn't quite long enough to measure the length of the space that it had to fill.

Simple. I just ran the rule out as far as it would go, made a mark, then used the rule to add the extra inches and made another mark. Then, with all the confidence in the world gained from having built a considerable number of boats, I picked up my handsaw and made my cut right through the *first* mark. Time out for expert boatbuilder cussing.

That's the kind of mistake you hope you will never again make. You swear you won't, but you very well might. Solution? Get a longer rule!

The same thing can happen with a folding extension rule, which is usually six feet long with a six-inch metal extension. I've cut a dory chine too short once or twice by putting the mark on the end of the rule instead of the end of the extension. Now I remember to take a hard look at where I'm putting the cutting mark, and to "tune in" on what I'm doing, at least for the critical moment.

Much the worst kind of mistake is the one that causes bodily injury. No one is immune. Familiarity with tools can be just as dangerous to the professional as unfamiliarity can be for the novice. I have had too many friends lose fingers in jointers and saws; they are men who have worked with such tools for many years. Talking with them usually reveals that inattention, distraction, or maybe a dangling sleeve was at fault. It's better to make all your mistakes on a piece of wood.

GIVE FULL ATTENTION TO YOUR PLANS

In my career of selling plans from South Thomaston to Singapore, it has taken a long time to have, finally, some boats being built from them in my locality. For some reason I'm not sure of, people right in my own community seem to be the last to know that good plans are available almost in their own backyard. Anyway, now that they've discovered my services and are taking advantage of them, it has been fun and very instructive to drop in on some to see what and how they are doing.

One of these is my close friend and good neighbor Dennis Hansen of Spruce Head. He had never built a boat before he decided to have a try at the Instant Boat Surf. He bought a set of plans in the winter, expecting to launch in the spring. He got it built, but the launching was later than he planned. He seemed to be going along all right; his first booboo was minor. He cut the midship side-frame a bit short so that it didn't reach the top of the side. That happened because he ignored the word *about* in Bolger's set of numbered key instructions to the plans. This item called for a piece of wood *about* 15½ inches long. And *about* is exactly what is meant, because there is a slight bevel on the bottom of the frame that calls for a little more wood. My friend cut it exactly 15½ inches long, with the ends square, and when the bevel was cut, the frame was a bit too short.

The more boats you build, the cagier you become, and trying to figure out what the designer means by such words as *about* is part of the fun of building. I keep an architect's scale at hand for checking measurements such as that. Had Dennis laid one directly against the frame as drawn on the plan, it would have showed 15½ inches lying against the hull; then his eye would have told him that, because of the bevel, it would have to be longer.

Dennis's next booboo . . . but first let's look at the two women who bought a set of plans to build the 7 foot 9 inch Elegant Punt. The next thing I heard from them was a phone call: "We've got the chines and gunwales in place, but it won't go together."

That was a new one on me. "If you've got it that far along, how come it ain't together already?"

"Well, we thought it would be easier to nail and glue the chines and gunwales on the sides while they were flat on the floor. They went on easy that way, but when we tried to bend them around the frame and fasten them to the bow and stern, they just wouldn't bend. What happened? Why won't the sides bend like they're supposed to?"

The answer to that was easy. "Because you made a laminated joint, which is inflexible. Better start over again. Cut new sides, fasten them to the midframe and then to the bow and stern transoms, and *then* put the chines and gunwales on."

I often wonder if they ever did, but I haven't heard from them since then, so I'll have to go on wondering.

Back to Dennis.

DRAW IT FULL SIZE AND CENTER EVERYTHING

Next time I went back to check Dennis Hansen's progress, the sides of his Surf were fastened to the stem and stern. Everything was in good alignment fore and aft, so I stepped back to view her profile. Wait a *minute*!!

How come she has more sheer than she is supposed to have? Back for another look at her frames and frame spacing. They were okay for positioning on stations. But when we measured the frames top and bottom, the mistake was apparent: the top of the midship frame was six inches wider then the plan called for. This caused the sides to be forced out, giving her the exaggerated sheer and bottom rocker so obvious when you stepped back to take a look. (By the way, it's good to have enough room in your workspace to be able to do this.)

"If we saw her in two twice, I think we can save her," I said.

Dennis turned from a greyish-white to a beet red. "My God, really?"

"Yep," I replied. "That will do it. Take a handsaw and cut her right in two so that the rest of the web frame will drop out and leave just the side frames.

Then pull the topsides in to the width she's supposed to have, put the web frame back in, and scribe it to the side frames. Next, put a plywood gusset on each side of the frame to strengthen where she was cut, and she'll be back in shape again." Which we did.

Making a mistake like that was not new to me. I had done it myself when I was building Bolger's Folding Schooner, but luckily I caught it before the error was built into the boat. It didn't shatter me to make that mistake, or any other one, though I always hope not to do it again. What I always do on the spot is try to figure out how to avoid doing it again.

And right there, one of the virtues of the Instant Boats comes to the rescue: all the Instant Boat hulls have constant flare, which means there is no twist to the sides. All frames and bulkheads lie at the same angle from chine to sheer.

Keeping that in mind, first draw a straight line on a piece of plywood or on the floor, and call it the centerline (⊄ on the plans). Next, draw another line at a right angle to that one, near the end of the first line, and let that represent the bottom of the frames—all of them. Now you can draw each frame, measuring out from the same centerline and on the same bottom line. Unless you have mismeasured, the sides of all the frames will look parallel to one another, just by inspection, and will prove to be parallel when you check them mathematically. If one of them isn't, it will be obvious. Now that the full-size drawings are right there in front of you, it is a simple matter to build the frames right on them—laying the actual pieces of wood in place just as they will go together. That way, you won't have to saw your hull in two.

THE TOTALLY UNSKILLED BUILDER

Now I'm going to lean pretty heavily on one of my favorite amateur builders, Lance Gunderson of Cambridge, Massachusetts. On his way from rowing his Gloucester Gull dory in the annual Rockport, Maine, Great Dory Race, he stopped by to pay me a visit. I invited him to go for a sail in the 20-foot 9-inch Zephyr. We met Dennis Hansen in his Surf and made something of a race of it.

Now Lance is a tremendously good classical guitar player, a rugged dory rower, and best of all, a totally unskilled boatbuilder—just exactly the kind of person Phil Bolger and I were looking for to build an Instant Boat. I was overjoyed when he said he'd like to take a crack at building his own boat. I knew soon enough this was the right man when we were sitting out on the lawn having a cold beer and discussing the building of a boat.

"How do you saw the chines out?" he asked.

"You saw them out of the clearest 2 x 4s you can find," I said. "You bevel them to whatever the angle is between side and bottom rather than saw them out square-edged. That way you save work by not having to cut the square edge off so the bottom will fit down flat. Let the tablesaw do the work."

"What's a bevel?"

There's no doubt about it, we've bought the right man, I thought. If he can do it, anybody can.

Besides, Lance had the determination. His hands were still sore from the 14-mile race he had just finished. He was the only solo rower in the whole fleet. Even so, he came in fifth or sixth out of 15, and he had hung in there and finished.

Let's read some of his firsthand reports on what he ran into while building his Surf. Every once in a while, I'll stick my oar in. Here's a letter dated September 2, 1977:

> Dear Dynamite:
>
> I think the hardest task so far has been putting those skids and the center shoe on alone. The shoe was warped, which made it all the more difficult. I had to use what was available, and the result is that the shoe is a bit crooked.
>
> If she won't row or sail well, I'll take it off and put on a straighter one. The fiberglassing was also a pain in the———. I'll never do any of it again.
>
> It seems to be taking forever for the final coat to harden, but took only a few seconds for it to become one solid mass in the milk carton I was using as a container. . . . Although epoxy resin is more expensive than polyester, it is, I think much easier for the novice to use, and it's pretty hard to goof it up, which certainly isn't so for polyester.
>
> I coated the inside and outside with Gluvit [an epoxy sealer]—trying to save the cheap Japanese plywood—now Gluvit is no great shakes either, at any rate I had to do something to seal the plywood, and Gluvit seemed the cheapest way. Now this business of always trying to find the cheapest way is ending up costing me MUCH more than if I had gone first class in the first place. [Right on! Incidentally "what was available" for the shoe turned out to be pine, not the fir the plan called for.]
>
> I have literally made at least one mistake on every number on the plan, the most disastrous being not noticing that the forward bulkhead frame slipped aft on one side almost an inch while I was trying to nail it. The result seems, and I stress the "seems," to be that only the original centerline is out of whack. A new one, the current one, seems O.K. Also, and I haven't figured this one out yet, the bottom buttstrap is crooked by several inches. I didn't even notice it until I painted the Gluvit on the bottom. What a shock!
>
> It was perfect on the ground, but somehow wound up cock-eyed on the boat. Now speaking of this buttstrap, the measurement on the plans is incorrect; if it is followed, the buttstrap will

overlap each side a quarter inch, and has to be chiseled or somehow cut off. Also, the cutwater seems to be out of whack on the plans. Most notably, the width called for is 2 inches and the shoe is 1½ inches. Also, the overhead view doesn't match the side view exactly.

Check it out when you have time; probably I'm missing something. In a sudden fit of enthusiasm I made the rudder and leeboard from ¾-inch scraps my father had lying around.

There are a few things *I* haven't figured out about the above. One is the matter of *only* the original centerline being out of whack. Also, I haven't fathomed the mystery of the buttstrap that was perfect on the ground but cockeyed in the boat, and why the mistake apparently didn't show up until Gluvit was being applied. A little more use of the scale and a little more step checking might well have been in order. And I'd like to flash a *Caution* signal on sudden bursts of enthusiasm: The plans make no mention of using scrap plywood that happens to be lying around (especially plywood of the wrong thickness).

I estimate I could have built the boat twice as fast with the aid of decent tools and a shop. Most sorely missed was the bandsaw. I got the rabbeted cutwater sawed out by a friendly apprentice for free after much hassling at the local boatyard. One "master builder" wanted to charge me $8.00 to do it. The job took all of 30 seconds (I had it all marked out, too).

I have used a spokeshave, hammer, large and small squares, block plane, tapemeasure, chalkline, compass and bevel, bastard file, Surform (which goes dull extremely fast), bit brace, screwdriver, four 6-inch C-clamps, architect's rule (which I don't see how you can build the boat without, since so very many of the measurements are not on the plans), electric drill, sabersaw, handsaw (dull), hacksaw (even duller), one-inch wood chisel (a great tool), and a drawknife, which I love to use. I guess that's a lot of tools. Oh, yes—I really missed not having a vise. This lack caused infinite delays, problems, and cursing. No one should attempt to build a boat without a vise! Build the vise first, then the boat!

I have to take exception to the importance of a vise. I find myself clamping almost everything to a sawhorse when working it—such an arrangement is convenient and portable. Sure, the vise is handy when you're chiseling and smoothing a shaped piece, but I wouldn't call it indispensable. As far as a dull saw is concerned, saws can be sharpened and new hacksaw blades can be purchased. This matter of sharpness is a fetish with me. All edged tools should be sharp. It ensures cleaner and more accurate work. And it ensures safety, too, when you think about it.

I had absolutely no experience with any form of carpentry whatsoever. I did read a lot of books, though. My favorites, those that were most informative: *Building Classic Small Craft* by John Gardner (International Marine Publishing Company); *Boat Carpentry* by Hervey G. Smith (Van Nostrand Reinhold); *Boatbuilding* by Howard I. Chapelle (W.W. Norton), a great book but useless for the Instant Boats as far as I can see; *Skiffs and Schooners* by R. D. Culler, *Small Boats* and *The Folding Schooner* by Philip C. Bolger (all three from International Marine Publishing Company). And of course the indispensable help from you, without which I never would have ever started!

Working alone is tough, and very discouraging at times, at least for me. My advice to any would-be Instant Boat builder is to get as much help as you can, especially BEFORE starting each piece. Working with ultra-fast-setting glues was very annoying to me. Always rushing to get everything together in time, and thereby making many little errors which compound easily. One can't trust the word of store salesmen on *anything*. Always ask a builder if you can.

. . . So far the Surf has cost me, including the sail, close to $400 in materials. A substantial saving could have been made by using one type of glue bought in large quantity. Epoxy is my choice, as it is reliable and easy to mix. Fastenings other than copper and bronze would save a lot ($6.00 per pound for copper nails!!), and knowing how to figure board feet, so that all lumber could be got at once and from the most reasonable source to cut down on those high milling charges the lumberyards are fond of demanding.

A good work space will surely cut down on mistakes, thereby reducing the number of ruined pieces. Planning well in advance would have saved more had I done it.

Obviously, Lance learned a lot on his first boat. But I would caution against wandering away from the materials in the plan specs. I'm thinking of the copper and bronze fastenings. They were specified for good reason and might well pay for their keep in making a sound and tight hull when the boat meets wind and weather.

Now comes the proof of the pudding, in a letter dated October 6, 1977:

Dear Paysons:

All in all I call my Surf, the *Shag,* a success; she's already given me enough pleasure to justify the expense and effort. She is not without idiosyncrasies; she refuses to go to windward. In a three-mile grudge race with a Banks dory and a Strawbery Banke dory, both with centerboard and spritsail, they beat the pants off me to windward, pointing much closer than I could. The ol' *Shag* just falls off and goes into a reach, or stops in irons. Man, is that embarrassing in a tight situation.

I wonder why she won't point up. It could be that the closet-pole mast is too flexible, but I doubt it, as she runs and reaches amazingly well, wiping out those dories every time with ease. In fact, when we raced, I arrived at the destination only a few seconds behind, though I had tacked dozens of times and they not at all.

It could be that I haven't sharpened the leeboard enough, although it's pretty fine to my eye. I doubt it's the sail, as it seems to fit well, is not loose, and snugs up nicely on the sprit boom. The rudder is very sharp and works perfectly; she is effortless to steer, with only a very slight weather helm, even in quite strong wind.

Doubt it's the warped shoe, as she rows much better than I expected, not yawing off course at all. In fact, I can even move her with the rudder and leeboard down and the sail up, as I had to do recently when the strong current of the Piscataqua River was dragging me toward a lee shore when the wind quit.

She seems to be in good trim too, riding right about on her waterline. But to windward she won't go. Could it be that big bowsprit's mast partner sticking out there? Did yours go to windward? Could it be that I haven't found the best trim? It doesn't seem that crucial in my experiences so far. She is really great on all other points of sail; I love to stand up when running, surveying the scene as she scoots along easily. She's a very stable boat; compared with the Gloucester Gull dory, what a difference a few inches of bottom makes!

Here we have a builder who loves his boat, even though she appears to lack one of the requisites of good sailing performance. His attempts to find a reason are instructive.

First, to answer the only question of his I can, at this distance: yes, mine points up, and so do all the other Surfs I have had the chance to observe.

Now I am not going to try a long-distance diagnosis, but I can say that none of his theoretical reasons appear to have any bearing on the matter. I'd need a firsthand, onboard examination and trial before I would venture an opinion. Lance's almost desperate reaching for an explanation is the typical amateur's approach. I would look for improper placement of one or more basic items—perhaps the mast, perhaps the leeboard, or possibly both. I look forward to investigating his problem.

Now, her second vice is perhaps more serious. That bowsprit won't hold the mooring line, with the result that she rides tied to the mast, easily swamping when heavy seas or motorboat wakes come by. Recently I got a call from the harbormaster in Kittery Point, Maine, where I had left her moored with mast in and sail tightly furled; seems my *Shag* was upside down, and everything that was in her—rudder, leeboard, bailer, etc.—was floating all over the Piscataqua.

By the time I got there, some kind soul had dragged her ashore, all covered with mud but intact. I rounded up all her gear washed up on nearby shores. No harm done this time. . . . . They tell me she floated on her side, about half out of the water, and would have righted without the mast. So, something must be added to keep the mooring pendant in place. I thought of just drilling a hole in the bowsprit and tying a painter there; or perhaps a sheave of some kind would do it. What do you think? If she still flips over once she is tied by the nose, then I shall have to take the mast out every time. What a drag. . . . Did your Surf ever behave like this?

No, my Surf never did. Again, inexperience has triggered an illogical search for a proper solution. First of all, she was never meant to be moored by the bowsprit. The solution is a ringbolt or some kind of shackle fitted just as low on the stem as you can reach to hang her pendant on. Then her bow won't be pulled down by the strain of the mooring.

Lance wound up his last letter with a set of plans and resolutions for any future boatbuilding activity, and possible modifications on his *Shag:*

I got a wicked infection from the fiberglass when I sanded it, itching like poison ivy. Edey and Duff, and Arthur Martin all say it's an occupational hazard. Well, it's enough to keep me from ever sanding fiberglass. . . .

Use thicker plywood throughout (*Shag* shudders in a frightening way when sailing into a head sea). . . . Economize on fastenings whenever possible. . . . Use two eye screws instead of the $15 pintles and gudgeons *Shag* now has. . . . Have sense enough to get Amy Payson to come down and help me put the shoe on (and use oak for it instead of pine). . . . Use epoxy glue throughout (it's worth the extra cost). . . . Work out some way to stow the oars inside the midship frame so they won't be in the way when sailing. . . . Re-read *The Folding Schooner* before commencing to cut plywood (there are a lot of hints hidden in there that would have helped me if only I had taken time to read that book). . . . Find a way to be able to remove the fore and aft decks so that things can be stowed there in addition to the flotation. . . . Remember to fill all nail dents with putty before painting. That's all I can think of to complain about now.

I think it's amazing that someone as ignorant as I am can borrow some tools, scrounge some lumber, and build a little boat as nice as this one in just about a month without pushing very hard. Other than windward performance, she far exceeds my fondest expectations.

I expect she will continue to be as much pleasure to use as she was to build. Certainly no boat could be easier to put together. Yet she works and looks far better than you'd expect. I've already had some compliments from goldplaters! One even recognized her as a Bolger design.

As you can see, beginners—and even pros—make mistakes, but it is from our mistakes that we learn. Lance Gunderson tried something he had never done before, and he is happy that he did.

4

Feet, Inches, Eighths
(It's the Rule)

Probably the one technique that most boat designers use in common is the "feet, inches, eighths" method of measurement on their plans. It takes a little time getting used to, but once you've got the system firmly in mind, it is quite easy to take any designer's plan and figure out any part of a boat with a good deal of accuracy, working from a table of offsets, which is a table that gives vital dimensions defining the shape of the boat. (Phil Bolger, on his Instant Boat plans, does not use the table format, however; the dimensions are drawn right on the plans.)

What seems to bother plan buyers the most is the eighths part of the system. Once they become accustomed to that, they are okay. The problem seems to be a number-set like 1, 5, 6. They know the 1 represents one foot and the 5 represents five inches, but they find the 6 bothersome because it represents six-eighths of an inch, and in ordinary carpentry, which is what they are used to, it would be called three-fourths of an inch. The same is true for a measurement of 1, 5, 4; the 4 is four-eighths or one-half inch. If the measure were 1, 5, 2, the 2 would be translated as one-quarter inch. The 2, 4, and 6 eighths are the unfamiliar ones we have to remember to translate. The rest of the eighths measurements—3, 5, and 7—are all familiar, because we use them in ordinary carpentry.

The numbers 1, 5, 0 represent one foot, five inches, and zero eighths—okay? But now you ask what the plus or minus signs alongside some of the eighths are for. Simple: just add or subtract $\frac{1}{16}$ inch, more or less, to modify the eighths figure.

31

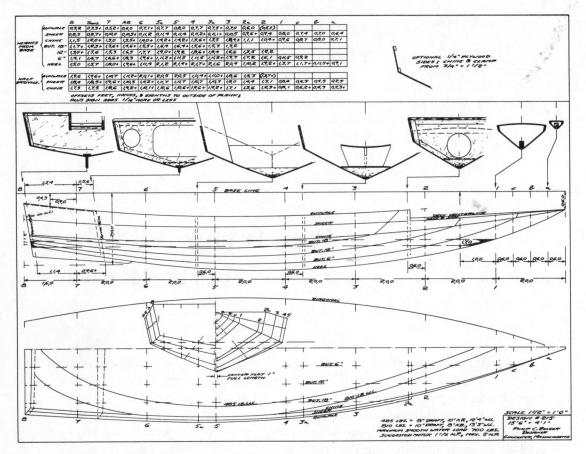

Lines and offsets for the Bolger-designed Thomaston Galley. Instant Boat builders can avoid lofting from offsets, since Instant Boat plans are all constructed by following numbered instructions.

It's obvious even to the dumbest of us when we look at a plan for a 30-foot boat that the boat isn't drawn full size. That's where the designer's artfulness begins. Say, for instance, he's drawn the 12-foot Instant Boat Teal on a piece of paper 22 inches long. He's scaled it down from 12 feet to about 18 inches so it will fit on his drawing board. The bigger he can draw it, the more accurate the drawing will be, but he has to be practical about it, because a 12-foot hunk of paper would be unhandy to lug around and unhandy for close-up viewing, too. So the designer scales the boat down to the size he has in mind, using an architect's scale rule, and settles on, in Teal's case, 1½ inches equals 1 foot, and he writes these numbers down in the little boxed section on the plan that carries his name and address.

Now, very often there is some loss of accuracy in laying down a fairly large boat to a small scale, so the builder uses a process called "lofting" to redraw the boat back to full size in three different views—profile, half-breadth, and body plan. This allows him to check the designer's drawings for any mis-measures and to make sure the curves are fair. Building the Instant Boats doesn't require that you know what the three views represent, but let's have a look anyway, to give you an idea of what you're missing.

The profile is a side view of the boat, the half-breadth drawing is a plan view, looking up at the boat from below, and the body plan is a sectional view showing the boat in cross-section, usually from the bow and the stern to amidships. All measurements start from a straight line called the baseline, from which you make height measurements, and another straight line called the centerline, from which you make width measurements. Believe me, this is about the simplest explanation of lofting as anyone can get, but the builder who gets a typical set of plans has to know much, much more, especially if he is building a round-bottomed boat.

If you want to pursue the art of lofting in depth, I suggest reading Howard I. Chapelle's book *Boatbuilding*, in which every refinement is covered in great detail, including "The Expansion of a Raking and Curved Transom." Luckily I never planned on building a boat that called for one, because that explanation went by me without slowing a bit.

The first thing the builder does after studying the general layout of the drawing is to see what scale the designer has used. Both the designer and the builder use the same rule, so the builder, knowing the scale and having the rule to measure it by, has the key that opens the door to understanding.

Let's pick up the scale rule and look at it. It's triangular in shape and has numbers reading in both directions. Tough, you say? Not at all. Just turn the rule around in your hand until you see the 1½ scale with 1½ on the left side of it. Note that the finely graduated 1½-inch segment is divided into 12 equal parts, with each of the longer marks designating an inch. Note, too, that this segment reads right to left, starting at zero. See the number 3? That's 3 inches; next is 6, then 9, and so on.

The 1½-inch scale is easy to read because of its rather large size, with the inch mark being divided into a half and then a quarter. But why do the numbered divisions on the graduated segment read from right to left? That's easy! Think of the graduated section as an extension rule for the other 1½

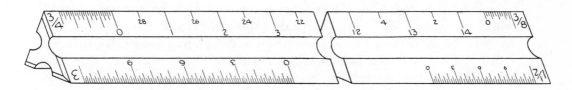

Architect's scale rule, open divided. (Reprinted from Mechanical Drawing, *7th edition, by T.E. French and C.L. Svenson, © 1966, with permission of Webster/McGraw-Hill.)*

spaces, then put the rule precisely on the third 1½ mark from zero, and let the rest of the distance being measured overflow to the left onto the graduated part. Say it lands on 6; that means your measurement is 3 feet 6 inches (if it's a little less than 6 inches, the reading has to be 5 plus whatever fraction it shows of the scaled inch).

Note, too, the 3-inch scale on the same face as the 1½ but on the other end. This can be used at the same time as the 1½ scale, because one-half of 3 is 1½, and using the 6 of the 3-inch scale plus the end gives you a couple more 1½-scale spaces for measuring. The rule includes a number of other scales, but I've never used the smaller ones under ¾ inch when building small boats.

Sometimes the designer uses more than one scale on his plans, depending on how much room he has and how much detail is needed. For instance, Teal's plans are drawn at the scale of 1½ inch equals 1 foot on two sheets, while the third sheet, the sail plan, is drawn on the ¾-inch scale because of the rather tall mast.

While making a model of Teal recently, exactly to the 1½-inch scale, I was rudely reminded how easy it is to forget how to think after a lengthy layoff from building. I had built the hull and was all ready to make the mast and sprit boom when I ran across the ¾-inch scale layout that gave the mast's height and dimensions as exactly half the size necessary to fit the hull. It took me a minute or so of stupid contemplation before I realized that all that was needed was simply to use the 1½ scale and lay out everything twice the size shown on the sail plan, thus bringing the mast back in proportion to the hull again. Nevertheless, my initial hesitancy came as quite a shock—to find that you've grown that dumb that quick can be painful. I'd like to think I can blame part of it at least on my 30 years as a commercial lobster fisherman, when to have an empty mind was the first requirement for being able to tolerate a roaring engine all day, to haul one stupid, lookalike trap after another was the next, and, as the final curse of the day, to face a couple of tubs of mushy, stinking herring to be stuffed, a handful at a time, into baitbags.

But we were talking about boat plans. For the amateur boatbuilder, a number of designers have drawn plans according to their ideas of what is easy to build. Out of curiosity I have sent for some, and others have been brought to me by prospective customers, so I've had a chance to look over quite a few different techniques and compare them with the Instant Boats.

Jack Betts of Wayland, Massachusetts, came to my shop one day lugging a roll of prints and a big box of tongue depressors as a gift. It was easy enough to see that the depressors would make great stirring sticks for small batches of goo, but the use of the plans was not as easy to figure out. They were for a small English plywood sailboat, with a V-bottom and the usual centerboard. The easy part of the plans, their most appealing feature from the amateur's point of view, was the full-size templates. What I found lacking was any step-by-step assembly process. With eight or nine sheets of big drawings scattered around, building the boat would have required more paper-shuffling back and forth than I have patience to endure.

Another set of plans arrived printed on both sides of a rather large sheet. This, too, was a small sailboat, with only a few steps required to build it. That sheet had plenty of information, of a sort; in fact, it had too much. Sections of the boat's construction were drawn here and there—but never to scale. Nor was there any view of the boat showing it complete. The payoff was the beginning of the instructions, which started with the quite unnerving words: "The basic steps to building [name of boat] *go something like this.*"

It may seem strange for me to say there is too much information on a plan, when the opposite is true of so many plans. But too much detail means that I have to keep all this clutter in my mind until I come to the place I need to use it. Because of mental laziness, I like a "read, cut, and fasten" method so I don't have to remember too much.

Like most people, I prefer to have my cake and eat it too, and I enjoy the feeling of being a rotten, spoiled kid that the Instant Boats give me. The reasons: The plans show the three views needed for clarity, they don't mention lofting, and they cover only a few sheets of paper. Best of all is the build-by-number approach, much like a paint-by-number coloring book. The novice builder is even spared knowing the name of the part he is making, and with marine terminology adding up to a language all its own, that can be a progress-stopper.

KNOW YOUR PLANS BACKWARD AND FORWARD

One of the best ways of getting to know your plans, and incidentally one of the best ways I know of learning to use the scale rule, is to build a model first before building the boat. There are substantial advantages to this procedure. Mistakes that might be made on the full-size version, where they can be very costly in time and money, can be caught and solved at the model stage. Material costs are just about nothing, as pieces of pine, cedar, etc., are often to be found lying around the shop. I've been tempted to use the balsa wood usually found in hobby shops because of the variety in sizes and thicknesses available, but I resist the temptation after comparing balsa's looks with pine and cedar. Some builders make their models from cardboard, which is plenty good enough just for seeing how the basic shape will look and how it goes together, but a cardboard model can't compete with a pine model sitting on the mantel.

I've made all my models from pine strips sawed out on an 8-inch tablesaw using a smooth-cutting planer blade to do the job. This saw will cut to a depth of only about 2 inches, so with a model that calls for, say, a 4-inch-wide bottom, the stock has to be put through twice, with the builder hoping to align

Above: *Pine-strip rigged scale models of, bottom to top, the Teal, the Surf, the Thomaston Galley, the Gloucester Gull dory.*
Below: *Scale model of the Teal, showing leeboard in place.*

the second cut with the first. It's safer to saw the stock a little heavier than wanted, using a sander to get it down rather than trying for exact size the first time.

Some of the tools needed for making models are 2-inch C-clamps, a fine backsaw like the kind made by X-acto, a small drill also made by them, a bunch of common pins, rat-tail files, a tiny block plane, and Elmer's white glue. I make no mention of paint, reflecting on my own attempts at painting models and what an ugly job I make of it. The above ingredients will produce a tolerably decent hull. For finer points, such as a professional paint job on a model, I'm waiting for Jay Hanna's book on modeling. Maybe it will give me courage to try painting one again.

THE ARMCHAIR METHOD

The importance of studying a plan and understanding it before you start drawing lines and cutting wood can't be overemphasized. The first consideration is *where* and *how* you start this familiarization process. There are two quite different approaches, as I see it. One is to crawl around out in the shop on your hands and knees, plans in hand, while you try to figure out how to shape and fasten something (a situation made even hairier if you find yourself trying to race a fast-setting glue).

The other method—and my choice—is in the comfort of an easy chair. No hurry; you can take a week of nights looking at the plans over and over, with scale rule in hand, trying not to miss a single thing. This way you won't be pressed, desperately trying to solve problems on the spot with the plans in one hand and the gluepot in the other. You have time to think out such things as what the designer meant by "the measurement is about 15 inches," which would have saved Dennis Hansen the trouble of making the side frame twice for his Surf.

At the same time, there are various parts of each Instant Boat that you can make first, if you prefer, while you are still figuring out how to build the hull. The rudder, leeboard, mast, boom, etc., can all be made without getting involved with the hull assembly process. Besides, I think it's a good idea to make a few parts first, because it gets the first-time builder acquainted with his tools and is a warm-up before the main event of getting the hull to take its shape. Even so, it's no big thing to get the hull to look just the way it's supposed to, especially since building is simplified by the easy-bending sides and bottoms of the Instant Boats, especially Surf, Zephyr, Schooner, and the Kayak. The more checkpoints there are for the builder to determine how his bulkheads, frames, etc., should line up, the easier and better the job will be.

Plans again. If you take your time reading the drawings, you will note a centerline indicated on every bulkhead, and temporary frame, and on the inside of the bottom. With careful attention to the alignment of the frames and the plywood bottom, any frame misalignment can be spotted either from forward or aft. It makes sense to draw the centerline on the outside of the bottom also, because the outside line will be used as a guide for putting the bottom shoe on the hull.

It's easy enough to figure how far from the edge to put your centerline on the plywood bottom. Just look at the widest frame in the boat, measure the distance from the outside edge of the chine to the center of the frame—and add ⅛ inch or ¼ inch all around, depending on how much you trust your sawing skills before you cut the outline of the bottom.

I don't think it is possible for a designer to develop a set of foolproof plans—plans that the ingenuity of the novice builder can't screw up. I am sure, though, that I can help foil this devilish ingenuity if I explain some of the really simple things, so simple that they are often ignored by designers and by experienced builders who try to teach the novice, because they are so simple to them that they assume everyone else must know. Subsequent chapters will develop some of those simple techniques.

5

Tools of the Trade

For me to list the bare minimum of tools required to build a boat is a little difficult; I have spent all my life trying to collect enough tools so that I can do any job within my capabilities the easiest and fastest way. This requires more than the minimum number of tools. It's a question often asked, though, by the novice, who wants to build only one boat and doesn't want to spend money on tools he may never use again. I can easily go along with the economy aspect after having a look at the present prices of even the simplest hand tools.

You can save money by keeping down the number of tools you purchase, but the other side of the coin is that the fewer tools you have, the more you will have to use your head and hands. For instance, you can saw out the chines and gunwales of an Instant Boat with a hand ripsaw (that's a type of saw with about seven large teeth to the inch, used to cut lengthwise with the grain). And while you're at it, for a closer fit of the bottom to the chines, you can tilt the saw just the right amount to put the bevel on two chines at once, assuming you have a board wide enough to get both chines from. Beveling as you cut saves some hand planing, which would have to be done if you sawed the chines off square-edged. My own choice of tool for that job would be a tablesaw or a portable electric circular saw, both of which allow you to set the saw at the correct angle. (I discuss power tools in more detail in the next chapter.)

THE BAREBONES TOOL CHEST

Besides the ripsaw, other non-power tools you'll need include a crosscut handsaw, a hammer, a small block plane, an eggbeater-type drill, a try-square (or combination square), an adjustable bevel square, a bit brace, and a steel retractable pocket rule up to 16 feet long. I do not doubt that a builder will find something missing from this meager list when he settles down to build his boat. I'm acquainted with that type of frustration whenever I do a job outside my shop, because I always manage to forget something—maybe I've cleverly packed tools for the more intricate problems I expect to meet, but when I reach for my hammer, it isn't there.

While we're on this saw and hammer business, I'm reminded of a common complaint of customers who come to my shop either for ready-built boats or sets of plans. It goes like this: "Boy, I'd like to build a boat like that, but I can't even drive a nail or saw a board off straight." What they don't know, and never occurs to them to ask, is why. If they wouldn't be so quick to blame themselves, they might, in time, find out that a good part of the problem could rightly be blamed on the *hammer* and the *saw*.

Tools of the trade include: drawknife, bit brace, spokeshave, matching plane, rabbet plane, chamfer plane, bullnose rabbet plane, interchangeable screwdriver, Yankee screwdriver, "eggbeater"-type hand drill, Screwmates, screwdriver bits, countersinks.

More boatbuilder's hand tools: architect's scale rule, extension rule, tape measure, screwdrivers, dividers, calipers, combination square, chalk line, two-foot framing square.

Still more non-power tools: cat's paw, wood rasp, half-round mill file, handsaw jointer, saw set, 13-ounce hammer, chisel, bevel square, low-angle block plane, wooden jack plane, 10-point crosscut saw, backsaw, C-clamps, nail tray (including a machinist's punch used as a nail set).

THE GOOD HAMMER

Even a professional can't do much better than the amateur with a dimestore-variety hammer. The cheap hammer is rarely hung properly. The head is usually set at close to a right angle to the handle. This causes the hammer face to strike a glancing blow and slip off the nailhead. A properly hung hammer has the head hooked back slightly, so when the heel of the handle is resting on a flat surface with the head down, the face of the head will rest nearly flat. The reason for this desirable design feature is obvious when you consider that your arm has a natural, slight bend when you strike a nail with a hammer. The hook of the head allows the hammer face to strike the head of the nail flat, while your arm is in a position that is as natural as possible.

There are two more faults that sometimes need correcting so that the hammer won't be a bother to the user. One is that brand-new hammers usually have perfectly flat faces. When you first bring a new hammer home, put it on a grinding wheel and round the face slightly. A rounded face on a hammer will set the nail slightly when it is driven, yet leave just a smooth dimple on the surface of the wood that is easy to fill. A perfectly flat face will break the grain of the wood and leave an ugly scar. Some carpenters prefer to drive nails in lightly and then set the heads fairly deep with a nail set. My choice is to sock the nails right in until I see the wood compress, and then set them just a little bit more.

Another common fault of many hammers is that their faces get too smooth after much use, and they tend to glance off the nailhead. Rough up the face of your hammer a little with a piece of coarse sandpaper, rubbing it sideways, or use a grinding wheel. Even a handy rock will do.

I keep three sizes of claw hammers in my shop: a 16-ounce one for heavy nails, such as 8-penny board nails to 20-penny spikes; a 13-ounce for driving nails 5- and 6-penny or less; and a 6-ounce to start nails in holes or drive brads. I also have a small ball-peen hammer for heading rivets, and 2- and 5-pound mauls for backing nails that are being driven into a bouncy surface. The mauls are perfect when nailing gunwales and chines onto a light plywood hull.

Driving a nail is so simple for the professional carpenter that he never gives it any thought at all. It's a natural reflex action, like breathing or walking: the nail is there, and a few healthy swings of a hammer drive it home. That's all there is to it? Well, not quite. For a view of how the novice does it, let's take a look into the Rockland Boat Shop, Rockland, Maine, back in the 1940s, where three lobsterboats are being built for three owners who are in a hurry to get them overboard and fishing.

In walks Axel Gronros, shopowner and master builder, who pauses for a moment on the loft overlooking the work area to check progress on the three hulls. He listens to all the hammers ringing—all, that is, but one. His practiced eye and ear spot quickly the offending workman who is "choking the hell" out of his hammer, holding it too close to the head, and as a result is striking only very light blows. Exasperated, Axel goes down to the man, takes the hammer out of his hand, goes over to the bandsaw, and cuts six inches off the handle.

"Here," he says, handing the lopped-off hammer back to the wide-eyed workman. "If you ain't going to use it, you don't need it."

I doubt if there could be any more effective way to convey the message Axel was trying to get across. Before you label him some kind of tyrant, I'd like to point out that this man would often drop whatever he was doing, start up his great bandsaw, and shape a toy boat right on the spot for any bright-eyed boy who happened into the shop, without regard to whether the kid's father was a customer or not. Axel has long since departed this earth, but he left behind scores of lobsterboats, some going back to the 1930s, all still fishing the waters of coastal Maine and serving as testimonials to his skill with tools and his ability to direct others in their use.

Novices often choke up on the hammer handle when they're first learning to use one, because that's the only way they can hit the nail at all, and if they miss the nail, there's no great harm to the adjacent wood or any fingers.

There isn't much to tell about learning to drive nails; the basics are simple. Buy yourself a good hammer and keep the face of it rounded and rough. Start the nail with light taps. Keep your fingers well out of the way, and then swing. As you gain confidence and strength, you will find that you are holding the handle closer to its end, you are missing the nail less frequently, and you are well on the way to becoming a pro. All it takes is time and practice.

THE SAW

Every boatbuilder's toolbox should contain at least four types of hand-saws—the aforementioned rip and crosscuts, and a coping saw and a keyhole saw for more intricate jobs than sawing a board in two. The coping saw can be used for sawing out circles within the range of its depth of cut, or for almost any kind of pattern, because its very small blade can be turned through 360 degrees in its frame. The keyhole saw is good for much the same kind of work, but usually its cut is rougher; however, it is not limited to any given distance from the edge of the work, as it has no frame.

Here I recommend a power tool: the electric sabersaw, which has just about ended the need for both the coping and keyhole saws. It doesn't even need a starting hole for cutting in the middle of a large piece of plywood. With a sabersaw, it's just a matter of tipping the blade nearly parallel with the wood and slowly bringing it to the vertical as the blade bites its way through.

The handsaw is commonly found in most households and shops in conditions ranging all the way from clean and sharp to useless, maybe kinked, or as we say in Maine, a bed of rust. Most people pick it up and saw through a board

Handsaws: hacksaw, backsaw, coping saw, modelmaker's backsaw.

without thinking much about its condition. Then they discover that the cut is maybe half an inch off the line. This is where the difference between the novice and the pro shows up. The novice has perhaps sawed off only a few boards in his lifetime, with not a single straight cut to his credit, so he blames himself.

The pro has made plenty of good cuts right to the line, and he knows in an instant that when the saw starts running off, it's the saw that's at fault. How does he know? It's simple. The pro has taken the time to find out why some saws will cut straight while others won't. He turns the saw over and sights along the teeth. Aha! There's a section on one side of the blade where the teeth are no longer sharp but have been dubbed over from grazing a nail that he or the last user didn't see buried in the timber. The dull side drags while the sharp side still cuts; thus the saw is pulled out of line.

Or perhaps the saw has just come back from a saw filer who either doesn't know how to do a good job or doesn't care. If the teeth are shorter on one side than on the other, again the saw will run off the line. This is easy enough to spot in a crosscut saw: just sight lengthwise along the teeth from tip to handle. The teeth should appear uniform in height, and because of the "set"—the slight tilt of alternate teeth in opposite directions—should show a groove down the middle the whole length of the blade between this alternately right and left set of teeth. Actually, if the saw is filed properly, has the right amount of set, and is free of kinks, you can place a needle in the groove between the right- and left-set teeth, and when you release it, the needle will slide the whole length of the tilted blade in the groove.

44

DO IT YOURSELF: FIRST, THE SET

The best way to find out what makes a saw cut true is to file one yourself. The process is simple, but it takes a lot of practice beforehand and eye to develop the required coordination. I was lucky, because my father showed me early in the game how to sharpen every kind of saw from a fine-toothed backsaw to a 3-foot circular type for cutting firewood ... *after* I became so embarrassed about lugging all my saws to him that I finally asked him to teach me how. Today, the danger is real that good handsaw filing will become a lost art. Here's a quote from *The Mariner's Catalog, Volume 5* (International Marine Publishing Company) captioned, "Sadder But Wiser Are We":

> Time: Last week
> Place: Sears, Roebuck Store, Topeka, Kansas, hardware department
> Me: "Do you have a saw set?"
> Them: "Oh, no, they're all sold separately."

So you're not the only person who never heard of a saw set.

I suppose reading about it won't make an expert saw filer, but let's give it a try. We'll start with a 10-point (10 teeth to the inch) crosscut. First, if it's rusty, get that rust off. Next, "joint down" the teeth so they're all the same height. This is done with a tooth jointer, a small metal device about six inches long in which a file is set. You rub the jointer over the teeth from the heel to the tip of the saw a few times; this very effectively flattens the tops of the teeth.

Next comes the set of the teeth. So the saw will not bind in the cut, the teeth have to be wider than the thickness of the blade. (Some of the better grades of saws are made with the blade tapered so that it is thicker near the teeth and thinner on the top edge, which helps the blade clear as it makes the cut.) We use a small handsaw "set" for this, which regulates the amount of set each tooth is given by the use of a dial or wheel typically calibrated from 0 to 11. Rotating the dial adjusts a tapered metal anvil up or down in relation to a piston-type plunger. You put the tooth between the anvil and the plunger and squeeze the tool's handle. The plunger pushes or "sets" the tooth sideways.

The amount of set a saw needs to cut properly takes some knowledgeable guessing, along with some understanding of the traits of wood. To cut soft, green wood requires a saw with more set, and to cut dry wood, whether hard or soft, needs less. A saw with too much set, used with dry wood, will rattle in the cut and make it rough. Too little set in a saw used with green wood will make the saw bind, at times so much as to make the cut impossible. You can tell whether or not the set is right by the saw's performance.

Putting more set in a saw is simple enough. Just set every other tooth on one side of the saw, then repeat on the other.

DO IT YOURSELF: FILING

Now that the teeth are jointed and set, it's time to begin filing. But before you grab a file and start in, let's examine what we're looking for in a properly shaped tooth. For a crosscut saw, the front of each tooth should slant back about 15 degrees, the back of the tooth should slant back about 45 degrees, and the edges should be beveled about 24 degrees. Send 25 cents to Disston, Inc., 601 Grant Street, Pittsburgh, Pennsylvania 15219—attention Cynthia Ser. You'll get a pamphlet that shows the saw teeth in nice, big, clear illustrations.

We can translate the specified degrees in simple, practical terms. If the front of the tooth pitches ahead or stands closer to the vertical than the Disston illustration shows, the tooth will bite deeper than it can chew, and the blade will bounce and chatter. If, on the other hand, the tooth leans back too much, it will just slide over the board and do little cutting.

Now put the saw in a filing vise and select the proper file. For a 10-teeth-to-the-inch saw, a 7-inch, extra-slim-taper, 3-cornered file is best. Stick a wooden handle on it and start filing.

Start from the tip and work toward the handle, without regard to which side comes first. Hold the file tilted toward you about 20 degrees and angled back about 25 degrees to the blade, and push the file through, between the teeth with the set of the tooth (that is, with the tooth leaning away from you). Keep the top of the file as flat as possible and do not let it roll either to the right or to the left. File two teeth with one stroke—the file will hit the front of the tooth set away from you and the back of the one ahead. Watch the teeth carefully, and avoid getting either tooth to a sharp point the first time across.

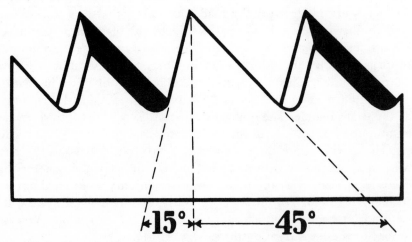

Detail drawing of crosscut saw teeth, showing the proper angles: 15 degrees for the front face, 45 degrees for the back. (Courtesy Disston, Inc. Reprinted with permission.)

File one side, then turn the saw around, and, still holding the file the same way, repeat the process—*this* time bringing the teeth to a point.

When you are first learning to file, it's hard to tell whether or not you have filed too much off, because the file leaves a burr that hides the point. Just tap the tooth with the wooden handle of the file; that will knock the burr off and will quickly show whether you have filed the tooth to a point or not.

Once the saw is filed and out of the vise, lay it on one side and *lightly* run a file on the side of the teeth, evening up the set and taking off the burrs.

A word of warning: in recent years various devices have come on the market supposedly to make saw filing child's play for everyone. Enticing as they seem to be, in my experience no machine can produce the equal of a hand-filed job.

BEVELS ARE IMPORTANT

Collecting and using small tools is a favorite hobby of mine, and through the years I've collected many, some of which turned out to be quite useless, and others I wouldn't like to think of doing without. Take the bevel square, which is frequently useful in boatbuilding: it comes in handy right from the start, since it is used to take bevels off the plans.

The bevel square is simple enough to use. For example, to find the bevel on one of the bulkheads of an Instant Boat, just lay the bevel square right on the plan, keeping the handle parallel and snug to the bulkhead while you swing the blade until it is parallel with the side of the hull. Then lock the tightening screw so the blade won't slip, pick up your bevel board, and run the square up or

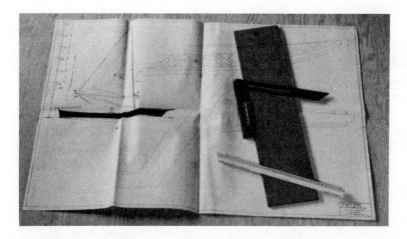

The bevel board (under the bevel square and the scale rule) is made of plywood and marked off with all the angles that might be needed for making bevels on an Instant Boat.

down it until the angle on the bevel square matches an angle marked on the board. That's the angular degree of the bevel you're looking for. Crank your saw table, Skilsaw, handsaw, or whatever, to that angle, and you are ready to cut wood.

Fine, you say, but what's a bevel board and where do you get one? You make it yourself, out of a piece of plywood ⅜ inch thick, 5 inches wide, and 20 inches long. Use either a protractor or the miter gauge on your saw, and lay the bevel square on it. Starting with zero, mark each angle of degree up to 45 degrees, starting them about one-quarter inch apart on the board.

Simple as that? Not always. There are two places where the bevel gauge will lie to you, no matter how careful you are. Those are the half-breadth plan views of the stem and transom (looking up from the bottom of the boat, remember?). No need to panic, though, because the designer knows you can't take off those bevels that way, and if he's being good to the builder, he will draw another version of them in cross-section at right angles to the stem and the transom, which will give the right amount of bevel.

Here's why you can't take the stem bevel off the half-breadth plan view: Let's use the 12-foot Teal as an example. If you measure the fore-and-aft stem thickness on the profile view, you get a thickness of 1½ inches at the cross-section. But if you measure the top of the stem on the half-breadth view where the sheer has cut it and the rake of the stem has tilted it, you will get a measurement fore and aft of 1⅞ inches. This makes a longer bevel on the stem, and a false one, since, in order for the sides to fall into a fair curve to meet the stem, the bevel has to be taken off at a right angle to the face of the stem.

The designer often shows a full-size view of the stem with the sides of the boat attached and with the proper bevel. Checking the angle of the sides in this view against their appearance in the half-breadth view shows quite a difference. How this can affect the looks and shape of the boat hull is quite interesting. If you do it the wrong way and lift bevels off the half-breadth view, you have an *under*-beveled stem, which draws in the sides and causes a bottle-necked appearance viewed from fore and aft. At the same time, drawing in the sides ruins an otherwise graceful sheer by throwing a hump into it.

I know this is frustrating, because it has happened to me. It is especially frustrating when the stem has been nailed and glued to one of the sides, and the glue has already set up. You go to fasten the other side and find the bevel is off by a mile (well, it seems like a mile). If you should ever make this mistake, don't nail the second side on: saw out another piece of wood to fill the gap, glue it on, and nail it to the stem; *then* nail the side on and keep going.

Just a small amount of under-beveling will spoil the looks of a boat, so my practice is to *over*-bevel when in doubt. Either on the stem or the transom, a small amount will leave only a small gap to the outside to fill and won't ruin the boat's looks.

The stern bevel presents the same problem as the stem, but to a lesser extent.

It is larger to work with, so there is less chance of "wobbling" the work when pushing the wood through the saw.

I ran into a little trouble with the stem of Teal, but I attributed that to careless measurement. Then, with Zephyr, I found the stem was way the hell off, so I wrote Phil Bolger. He sent me back corrected bevels with the remark, "This is what I mean by responsible updating." That has been an important part of our partnership in the Instant Boat concept. Once again, however, I would like to emphasize that it's usually a mistake to blame the designer.

I am quite leery of calling wolf too soon, and here's an example of when caution was justified. It might also cheer you a little to find out just how stupid a mistake a pro like me can make. I was building the first Teal, and, being extra careful, I marked the two temporary frames "fore" and "aft" so they couldn't possibly end up reversed. I cheerfully went ahead and placed the widest of the two frames aft and the narrower one forward, hardly thinking about it, because that's the way they always go (except in this boat).

Assuming the frames were in the right place cost me a good deal of anguish, trying to pull the sides in so they would rest just right on the sternpost. I was so sure that I hadn't made a mistake, I nearly called up Phil to tell him that this one just wouldn't go together. Luckily I didn't, because the reason soon became obvious. I had stupidly marked the frames on an *assumption* of how they were supposed to go instead of what the measurements clearly told me I will likely continue to make mistakes as long as I can swing a hammer.

THE HAND PLANE

So far we've concentrated on the more basic tools needed to build an Instant Boat. Now let's look at some others, starting with hand planes. Of all the different types of planes I use, I find the small, low-angle block plane the one I reach for the most. It's light and untiring to use, even though you may find yourself using it over quite a long period of time. As the name implies, the cutting iron is at a low angle to the work, so the plane is good for working with cross-grain and has little tendency to chatter or to tear the wood, as some of the other types of block planes do that have irons at a steeper angle. I'll plug two manufacturers: Stanley and Millers Falls make the best planes.

Even the best planes have to be sharpened from time to time, and here is how to go about it: Use an oilstone—the bigger the better—say, about 9 inches long and 3 inches wide. Saturate it liberally with kerosene, and, holding the iron as close as possible to the angle at which it sits in the plane, move it back and forth in a long, leisurely figure-eight or in a straight back-and-forth motion. Do this until you feel a burr on its edge.

Now turn the iron over and, with it flat, or nearly so, take a few light strokes over the stone to get rid of the burr. Then take another stroke or two back in the first position, and the iron should be sharp. To keep the proper bevel, bear in mind that the bevel should be about twice the thickness of the iron itself. The same rule applies to chisels.

I'm not fussy about the type of oilstone that I use, except that I like one with a coarse side and a fine side. What does matter is having the stone set on the bench so it doesn't slide around while you are using it. You can take care of that very easily by burying the stone in a piece of wood. Drive brads into the bottom· of the case, and then cut them off and sharpen them. The stone will remain stationary in use.

I remember an artist who stopped off to visit my shop while I was sharpening a plane iron. He took one look at me free-handing the hell out of the iron on my old swaybacked oilstone, and—being some kind of perfectionist, I suppose—said I was ruining the shape of the edge because the way I was sharpening it was bound to round the iron so it would hollow the edge of a board rather than make it flat. He went on to describe a device on the market (which I had already seen) that holds the iron in a fixed position, and, with a built-in roller, guides the iron very precisely over a stone that presumably is precisely flat. I didn't see fit to tell him that an iron sharpened that way is good only for the edge of a board, and that is all. Used in the middle of a wide board, sharpened straight across like that, the outside edges will dig in and make a mess of the job.

Devices like that bother me because they aren't needed. They hinder progress, and even worse, they tend to destroy whatever confidence a novice builder might be developing in his own hand and eye. Don't get me wrong; I'm not against gadgets. I like them very much, but only when they make sense to use. As for that particular gadget, I hope someone will lug a bushel basket of them into my shop, so I can have the pleasure of lugging them to the town dump.

The block plane is about the smallest plane you'll find in any carpenter's tool chest. For heavier work, it's good to have a jack plane or smoothing plane that is a foot to a foot and a half long. I like the wooden one best if there is much planing to be done, because it has less drag than the metal ones. The only drawback to the old wooden types is that the iron has a tendency to go out of adjustment after you strike a knot. Whacking the plane with a hammer to adjust it doesn't appeal to me, yet that's the only way it can be done. As a matter of fact, my wooden smoothing plane does have an adjustable iron, but it's the only one I've ever seen. If you should find one, latch onto it. I'm very fond of mine and am always delighted to have a chance to use it and to watch the long, unbroken shavings it peels off.

Though you won't need one to build an Instant Boat, a rabbet plane belongs in a builder's complete collection. You can make a groove with it, and, because the iron is flush with the outside body of the plane, you can use it to plane right up close to another surface that you don't want to cut, or right up to anything that's in the way. There's nothing to take its place if you have such a job to do by hand.

While we're on the subject of taking off wood, especially if you are in a hurry or you want to save sandpaper when rounding off corners, there are two files I wouldn't be without. One is a 10-inch carpenter's rasp, and the other is a 9- or 10-inch half-round file. Both have flat and rounded sides. The rasp has coarse teeth and will take off wood in any direction, regardless of grain, faster and better than the Stanley Surform, and it stays sharper longer. The half-round file is finer toothed and can be used to smooth the work after the rasp and still save on sandpaper. The rasp and the file are far less awkward to use because the handles are *in line* with the file blades, rather than offset as is the Surform.

THE BIT BRACE

The bit brace serves a double purpose for me—boring holes and driving screws. My choice of bits starts with one-quarter-inch and goes up by sixteenths to one inch and more. If you can get them, Russell Jennings bits are the best. They have a fine starting worm that holds better than the coarser ones, and it feeds the bit into the wood slowly and evenly without tearing itself out.

About the only thing to watch for in boring a hole, other than trying to keep the bit as straight as possible, is allowing the bit to break out on the underside of the hole. Stop boring when the worm shows through, then turn it over and bore the other way—or, if space won't allow that, clamp a piece of scrap behind the wood and bore into that.

I seldom bore anything today by hand if it can be done with power, so I mostly use my bit brace now for driving screws. Years ago, a screw-driving device that fitted a one-quarter-inch drill came on the market. The first ones had no tension-sensing capacity, and as my drill wasn't a variable-speed job, the results were disappointing to say the least. In softwood the screws would drive right out of sight with one press of the trigger, and in hardwood they'd break off. There went any dreams I might have had of mass-production efficiency. There was another bad habit that rig had—the driver would jump out of the screwhead slot and gouge up the surface I had spent hours making smooth.

For the number of screws I drive now, using a screwdriver bit in my hand brace is just fine. Moreover, I can feel just how much tension is being put on each screw in whatever kind of wood it's going into. It only takes four different sizes of screwdriver bits to fit any screw from under 1-inch number 10s to over 2-inch number 14s.

Along with the bits, it's desirable to have a selection of Screwmates (made by Stanley), which drill perfect holes for wood screws. There's one for just about every screw size. They have countersinks on them, but in plywood, be

An extensive collection of drills and bits.

careful to drill only as far as the countersink—never countersink in plywood; leave the compression strength there.

There is another type of Screwmate made by W.L. Fuller, Inc., of Warwick, Rhode Island. They're better because they can be adjusted to fit longer or shorter screws in the same wire size, and they have an adjustable counterbore as well. However, they're too expensive to have many lying around. Mine fits a number 10 wire screw of about any length, but I use it mainly for 1¼-inch screws, the size you'll find you'll use most commonly in building an Instant Boat. Such a screw, for instance, will fit the Wilcox-Crittenden oarlock socket number 4482 and their ½-inch gudgeons number 462, and many other places where a screw is handier than a nail.

A word of warning: There are a number of devices to make holes larger than the bits you customarily use for hand boring—some are good and some are not, depending on the size hole you want, the depth it must go, and how hard the wood is. One of these is the expansion bit, invented in 1890, which bores a hole from ¾ inch to 1½ inches and is adjusted by sliding a cutter in and out to the side. It's still on the market but should have been given a decent burial long ago in view of what's available now.

Another adjustable bit is a circle cutter with a ½-inch-diameter round shank to be used in a drill press; it is adjustable from ¾ inch to 7½ inches. It is okay as long as you use it only in a drill press; to use it freehand in an electric drill is to invite chaos, if not mayhem. Just the slightest amount of wobble will cause the cutter (mounted outboard on an arm) to dig in, which will break the device . . . or, if the workman is using a heavily powered drill, it will turn him into a corkscrew.

The best hole cutter I know of is the hole saw made by Black and Decker. Cutters are available for each hole size, and they will cut more than an inch deep when used in both directions. To have an array of these in various sizes means quite an outlay of money. The important thing is that they will do the job well and safely for the operator. Another manufacturer offers a whole cluster of hole saws all on one shank, which looks like quite a bargain. This outfit is too lightly made to stand any hard cutting (I proved that).

HOME MADE TOOLS

The old saw about necessity being the mother of invention certainly holds true for boatbuilders. Often, as you will find, you'll need a special tool or an extra pair of hands right when you're in the middle of doing something. I'll give you three examples of tools that have helped speed and ease my work.

One tool is the homemade sanding block. Getting a fair curve on the chine is hard to do after the bottom has been put on. This is because plywood has both hard and soft grains in it. The result is that you get dips when the plane hits soft grain and high spots when it hits the hard grain, which it tends to slip over rather than cut. The same thing happens when you are trying to sand plywood with the usual short sanding block; the outside curve of the chine makes the chore that much harder. The solution is very simple: Make a sanding block long enough to span the soft spots. This is easy enough to do by using some of the wood that is always lying around the shop. I made my block so it would take a discarded 3-by-21 sanding belt. I cut the belt where it is joined together and brought the ends over on top of the board. Nails or staples can be used to fasten the paper to the block.

Again, the grain problem makes it hard to cut a perfectly round and smooth hole in plywood. But you can make your own sanding drums that will fit your electric drill. They'll do the job and cost next to nothing. First saw a ¾-inch or 1-inch piece of board slightly smaller than the size of the circle you want. Then make a flat place on the edge about one inch long. In the middle of this flat place, make a saw cut toward the center of the circle, going in about one inch. Now you can tuck the ends of your sandpaper into the slot. A couple of staples or nails driven into the flat place will hold the paper on your homemade drum and allow clearance between the fastening and the work being sanded. Here

A set of homemade sanding tools: sanding board, several sizes of sanding drums that attach to an electric drill, rubber-based sanding block, sandpaper.

Wooden "fingers" (sometimes called a spring stick) clamped to board to prevent saw chatter. A second set of fingers is clamped to the fence for precision work.

again, I prefer an old, used sanding belt to sandpaper. For the shank, a ¼-inch stovebolt three or four inches long will do fine. Bore a ¼-inch hole in the center of your drum, put a washer on the bolt, snug up to the bolt head, and shove the bolt through the hole. Put on another washer, add two nuts, tighten the rig up, and you're in business.

Few devices work as well as the human hand for holding objects just the way you want them, but here is a device that works better, in one set of special circumstances: It's a simple set of "wooden fingers" used to hold work against a saw-table fence when you're cutting long pieces or doing fancy work where saw chatter or molding marks can't be tolerated. Sawing freehand will almost always produce marks no matter how carefully you hold the work against the fence; but two sets of fingers, one of them clamped to the saw table and placed against the work with a little side pressure, and the other clamped to the fence with down pressure, will hold the work steady enough so that the finished cut will look as though it came from a factory.

To make your extra fingers, almost any short piece of board about a foot long and about five inches wide will do. Cut off the end at about a 35-degree slant (nothing fussy) and make a series of close, parallel end cuts (the "fingers") that are flexible, and that's it. This set of fingers works just about the same way as a jam cleat on a boat. You can shove the work through, but you can't pull it back until you release the pressure.

There are many more gadgets that can help make work easier and more accurate. Some you can make, some you must buy. We've discussed only a few here, but all of them are useful. Of the basic tools required, not even a Scrooge could complain of the cost of this minimal boatbuilder's tool chest.

6

More Power to You

Hand tools are fine if you're building a boat only for yourself and there's no hurry. But if you want to speed the process, you'll want power. If later on you decide to build professionally, you will have to use all the power tools you can get your hands on and learn to use them as fast and as efficiently as the next builder.

THE TABLESAW

After many years of acquiring both hand and power tools, I have at last reached the point where I have enough of both to build anything I want to build. As my interest is in small boats, I don't need the heavier equipment, such as a thickness planer, a large bandsaw, and the like. For instance, rather than own a costly thickness planer, I have all my lumber planed at the mill to the thickness I want, and then I strip it up, either on a tablesaw or with a Skilsaw, using a combination hollow-ground planer blade.

Picking the right size tablesaw and motor depends on the size of the boat you are going to build and the kind of wood you will use. For the Instant Boats, an 8-inch tablesaw with a ½-hp motor will do. This is about the minimum for sawing out anything a little thicker than a 2 x 4. As for the maker, I would choose Rockwell as the best. A tablesaw is usually a lifetime investment, so you might as well go first class.

The combination planer blade can be used for either ripping or crosscutting on a tablesaw, and it is great for plywood because it has a minimal tendency to tear the wood opposite the entry side of the cut. Kept sharp and in good shape, it can saw an edge so smooth that minimal sanding, or none at all, is needed.

As good as a combination planer blade is for smooth cutting, it's still not without its faults. It's hard to keep the blade from wandering along the cut when you feed work through a tablesaw freehand, either because the lack of any set to the teeth tends to make it bind or because the saw blade sticks up too high through the stick. The latter trouble is easy enough to solve—just adjust the table height so the saw will come only slightly through the top of the board, and, in the case of a Skilsaw, adjust the blade so it doesn't protrude too much on the bottom of the cut. Some builders don't bother to adjust table height; it really doesn't matter all that much, as long as the work being pushed through is held steady by a rip guide—and obvious safety precautions are followed. But feeding freehand is another matter. When feeding freehand, it is essential that the combination planer blade be set no higher than just enough for the teeth to show through the work, or you will find you can't keep the blade from wandering along the line, especially if you are sawing to a slight curve. As long as you use the planer blade in dry and rather thin wood, it works fine. But try using it on a piece of green oak or spruce, or almost anything green and very thick, and you're all done.

Once, thinking I could have the best of both worlds, I set the teeth of a planer blade a very small amount, with the hope that it would cut green wood without binding and still produce a reasonably smooth cut. True, it didn't bind anymore, but neither did it produce a smooth cut; I gained nothing by it. I might just as well have used a ripping blade in the first place; it would have cut faster, at least.

Unlike the planer type of blade, which always has the same tooth pattern of crosscutting teeth or rakers, the circular ripsaw can have either many or few teeth, and those teeth can be either large or small. It has been my experience over the years that the blade with fewer, larger teeth cuts much faster and

Power saw blades: crosscut blade, combination planer blade, ripsaw blade.

better than one with more and smaller teeth, especially in green wood. This applies to bandsaws, too. For instance, I used regular bandsaw blades with quite fine teeth for years, with only fair results, until I finally happened onto skip-tooth bandsaw blades with tempered teeth. They made quite a difference, both in ease of cutting and ability to stay sharp. Those are the only kind I buy now, and I always ask for the ones with the fewest number of teeth.

The planer and the rip blades will do all the power cutting you need for any of the Instant Boats. Like handsaws, they should be picked with an eye for quality. Some of the planer type are made too thin and heat rapidly when being run through a stick; this causes them to distort so much that they begin to wobble, which makes it impossible to finish the cut. That's the kind of blade you will find at the bargain counter—cheap but useless. I think it is better to spend money on a reliable brand-name blade and know what you're getting.

FILE IT YOURSELF

I feel precisely the same way about filing power saw blades as I feel about handsaw blades. It would delight me to know that I had succeeded in encouraging a reader to pick up a file and learn to do his own power blade filing. I would feel this way because it would mean that the worker who has already developed a close relationship with his hand tools would gain the same understanding of how his power saws work. There is a great deal of satisfaction in using a saw that really cuts, and in knowing what you did to make it do so. The point is that whatever you do to the saw, for better or for worse, the fact that you did it yourself is what matters. Gradually, by trial, error, and patience, you will come to understand what your saw is trying to tell you, and you will be able to do something about it.

I feel particularly strongly about the worker doing his own filing after I have watched some fellow burn his way through a board with a trail like a snake's path. Often, his saw blade is not dull but needs only more set to give its teeth clearance so it won't bind and smoke. A good workman should carry a saw set with him on the job and know when to use it. Not knowing means extra work with a plane to make the line fair, and extra cost for whoever is paying for the job.

Here's an illustration of how little attention is often given to a saw and the using of it. I was on a carpentry job on Spruce Head Island, working on a summer cottage. Lunchtime came, and the artist friend of the fellow I was working for asked if he could use my circular saw to rip a 2 x 4 while I was gone. "Sure," I said, "but you'll have to take off the blade that's on it and put the rip blade on."

When I came back, I could see he had ripped up the 2 x 4, but he wasn't looking very happy about it. From the cut he had made, it was easy to see why.

The saw had burned its way through with the familiar snaky trail.

"Your saw doesn't cut worth a damn," he said.

"Really? That's strange, it worked all right earlier this morning."

A glance at the saw showed a badly burned blade; the dimwit had put it on backward and had used it that way without knowing the difference. Putting a blade on backward is easy enough to do, but sawing that much without knowing what was going on—well, I found that a little hard to take. Knowing your saw is as important as knowing how to use your saw.

Filing the Combination Planer

The planer blade is hard to file because it has two types of teeth: crosscut and rakers. The crosscut teeth cut off a board, and the rakers do the job of splitting it lengthwise. The rakers are filed 1/64 inch shorter than the crosscut teeth.

Of course, before you do any filing, the teeth must be jointed to a uniform size. You can do this right on the tablesaw. Lower the saw blade slightly below the table, place a file on top of the saw slot, and crank the blade back up again until it touches the file. Then hold the file down with one hand and rotate the saw *backward* by pulling on the drive belt, and the job is done. It's a job that needs a feather touch, taking only just enough off the tops of the teeth to make them even in height. Any more than that means more filing and reduces the diameter of the saw.

Before filing the crosscut teeth, the shape of the tooth should be quite clear in your head so you know what you are aiming for. In general, the shape of the circular crosscut tooth is the same as that of the hand crosscut saw tooth, except the face of the tooth should line up with the center hole of the saw instead of tipping back 15 degrees or so, as in the case of the handsaw.

The raker tooth should have the same shape as any power ripsaw tooth, but to get it 1/64 inch lower than the cutoff tooth is pure guesswork, unless you have a grinding wheel mounted on a movable arm with an adjustable stop. We'll assume you don't. In that case, the thing to do is to take a few extra swipes of the file to bring the raker teeth lower than the crosscut teeth.

Filing the Rip

The circular ripsaw isn't at all hard to file, and anyone should be able to do it. Again, it is of first importance to keep clearly in mind the shape of the tooth. Usually, on the jacket that a new saw comes in, there is a description of how the tooth is shaped and instructions on caring for the saw.

A straightedge placed along the leading edge or face of the rip tooth should follow a line that runs halfway between the center hole (the arbor) and the outside of the saw. The extended angle of the top and back of the tooth should form a line striking halfway between the bottom of the tooth (the gullet) and the top of the tooth preceding it.

Filers get into trouble by failing to pay attention to keeping the proper tooth shape, even with a simple ripsaw. A common practice—and a poor one—is just to give the saw a quick touch-up job. This is the lazy filer's way. He just sharpens the top leading edge because it's easy, and he can get away with it a few times with no apparent ill effect or loss of cutting ability. After awhile, though, the back of the tooth starts building up because of continuous filing on the top front, until the back gets higher than the leading or cutting edge. When the back of the tooth is higher than the front, it tries to do the cutting. At this point, the blade becomes useless for further cutting and just gives up.

To avoid getting the tooth out of shape, the proper way to file is to start the stroke with heavier pressure toward the back (keeping the proper slope in mind) and shape the tooth to a point with lighter pressure.

Ripsaws come from the factory with the teeth filed straight across. They cut well that way for straight ripping jobs, but they don't work as well for the occasional crosscutting that the user wants to do without having to change the blade. Just a slight bevel of five degrees or so, put on the back slope to the point, will do wonders in improving the crosscutting function; this bevel will not take away any of the blade's ripping capabilities, either.

Whether the saw is filed properly or not, in time the teeth will need gumming out. As successive filings make them shorter, the gullets or hollows between the teeth become so shallow they cannot hold and throw out the sawdust. At this point the saw begins to cut more slowly and run hotter, because the shallow gullets generate friction. Take a grinding wheel of the proper size to fit between the teeth and gum them out, again as close as possible to the shape of the original saw. I do not recommend that every filer do his own gumming, because it takes a special device to do it with accuracy, and the device is too expensive to make its purchase worthwhile. The best solution is for the builder to file his own saw and be able to recognize the need for expert attention when the time comes.

POWER SANDERS

The belt sander. For fast and heavy sanding, a belt-type sander should be used. The size of your pocketbook and the amount of use you expect to give the machine are the best guides to choosing the size and type to get. I find a 3-inch by 21-inch belt size handiest to use for long periods without tiring. If you're in a hurry and have good muscles, you might choose a larger and heavier model.

Useful power tools for the Instant Boat builder: belt sander, electric hand plane, sabersaw, heavy-duty vibrator sander, router, portable circular saw (often referred to as a Skilsaw).

In buying any kind of hand-held power tool, I look for balance and lightness first before I give much consideration to brand names. Just by picking up a tool at the store and hefting it, making a few working passes with it, you can judge pretty well whether your hands will be happy with it. But. . .

Twice I've put my better judgment aside and bought tools just because they balanced better than some of the brand-name ones. I got stuck both times. The first was a 3 x 21 belt sander I spotted at the local Sears store. (Some swear by Sears power tools; I swear *at* them.) It was so comfortable in my hand, I couldn't resist it. It also had a reasonable price and boasted of having bearings sealed for life. So I bought the sander and lugged it home. After less then 20 hours' use, the rear drive-wheel bearings gave up, causing the belt to slip off. So I took the sander back to the store, where I promptly found that the cost of fixing it would nearly equal its purchase price.

I'll never forget how the sun reflected off the sander's polished surfaces as it twisted and turned on its way down toward the bottom of what must be the deepest flooded quarry in the world—the Rockland, Maine, town dump.

Directly from the quarry I went to a Rockland hardware store owned by D. R. Call & Sons, a firm with a generation of house carpentry and general-tool experience behind it. When I asked Charles Call for his opinion on what would stand up to hour after hour of hard, continuous work, he passed me a Stanley that didn't balance as well as the tool I'd given the deep six. But the Stanley is still on the job, after smoothing the hulls of nearly a hundred small boats, and it's ready for more.

Using a belt sander without doing more harm than good takes a bit of practice. Always start the machine clear of the work, then bring it down as flat as possible—all the while keeping it moving either fore and aft or from side to side, both before and after it makes contact with the wood. To linger in one spot for even a fraction of a second usually leaves a depression that has to be gone back over and over again to get out. What's worse is to tip the sander on its side, even just a little; this causes a deep cut that is so difficult to sand out that it must be filled instead.

The orbital sander. Not as fast as the belt sander, but far easier to use, the orbital sander comes in several different sizes. Some have a fore-and-aft motion that doesn't leave the swirl marks of the ordinary orbital type. The smaller ones don't have enough power to do much of a job except for very light sanding. The one I have, and the best I've seen so far—I can really lean on it—is a Rockwell 505 finishing sander. It takes half a sheet of sandpaper and runs at around 10,000 rpm. It has a nice grip, I can use it a long time without tiring, and it won't heat up.

Fiberglass dust is hard on any sander—the belt type as well as the orbital—so after each use I get out of them all the dust I can.

The disc sander. The disc sander is the fastest cutter of them all. A powerful one like the kind used in automotive body shops with a really coarse sanding disc is the meanest sander I've ever used. It will cut through almost anything, and in a hurry, too. Repair work, such as getting an old planked boat ready for fiberglassing, is where the disc sander excels, and it will take off old paint scale, bolt heads, or anything else in its path, right down to bare wood. The disc sander is far worse than the belt sander for making gouges, however, so use it only to mow the surface down to where you want it. For finishing, use the belt or the orbital sander.

THE ELECTRIC HAND PLANE

You would think that after I deep-sixed the belt sander, I would have learned to steer clear of Sears. I probably would have, but a search for an electric hand plane in all the hardware stores in my area turned up zero. So as a last resort, it was back to Sears again to see what they had. I found a very nice-looking little electric planer that fitted my hand so well I knew it was the one. Along with it came a sharpening device that could be clamped on the planer shoe, so I could sharpen the blade professionally right on the spot. Right up my alley, I thought, as I lugged my new toy home, complete with its spare cutter and sharpening attachment.

Just like the belt sander, this planer had sealed, lubricated-for-life, never-need-attention bearings. It was perfect for what I had in mind, which was cutting the overlap of half-inch plywood dory bottoms. Because of the edge grain, this job was really tough to do with a hand plane; it always guaranteed me a good sweat, summer or winter. It wasn't many dory bottoms later, however, before the new electric plane gave forth loud shrieks and squawks. I tried ignoring them, because you couldn't grease the sealed bearings anyway. The squawks didn't stop, though, and as the bearings wore the cutter shaft, the cutter began to wobble, which gave the wood surface a highly undesirable washboard effect.

I took the thing apart and inspected it, and found the "lubricated-for-life" bearing as dry as unbuttered popcorn. Oh, there was grease in there all right, but not on the bearings or gears. Apparently whatever they used for grease wouldn't stay on the bearings but had thinned out and thrown itself clear. There is no way of knowing when you buy a tool with sealed bearings whether it is going to last or not, but I've given you two examples from the same source that didn't. Once you break the seal, there is no way I know of to repack this type of bearing. The best I could do was to swap the bearings around so that the tighter one bore on the cutting shaft. I'm still using it, but I have to drive a charge of oil into the bearing before each use. I'd like to replace the bearing, because the plane worked so well. But guess what? They don't make it anymore.

Back to my gripe. For a company that built its reputation on an ironclad guarantee on about everything they sell, I fail to understand why they won't guarantee a power tool for a reasonable length of time or fix it at a reasonable price.

THE ROUTER

The router is probably one of the most versatile of all the power tools on the market, and with the variety of cutters available for it, the jobs it can do seem almost limitless. If you want to make moldings, or write your name freehand on a board, you can do it with your router. The motor turns up at about 20,000 rpm, producing a smooth cut and cutting down work time to next to nothing. I use mine mostly for rounding off corners on gunwales and chines, a job that used to take quite a while with a hand plane and sanding block, but it's also nice to know that it will do any kind of rabbeting job I might want to do as well.

The router has only one fault, and I will have to share in the blame for that—the user makes it happen, by not paying attention to the cutter adjustment. For example, suppose I'm putting a ¼-inch or ⅜-inch round on a gunwale or chine. If I lower the cutter enough to do it all in one bite, quite often it will pick up a sliver and run it for two or three inches, thereby making me very unhappy. To avoid that, it's much better to start with a shallower cut and then increase the cutter depth in stages until you achieve the final depth you want.

THE BANDSAW

For most small shops, a 12-inch bandsaw is just fine. The 12-inch measurement is the throat distance—that is, the distance between the saw blade and the frame of the saw, which means you can saw something up to 12 inches wide. Mine is only a 10-inch saw, but it does a nice job of sawing, and with a sharp blade, it will cut through 3-inch oak. But it does sometimes break blades because of the small diameter of the wheels the blades travel on. As far as I know, the 12-inch and larger saws don't have that problem.

You can always tell when a blade is getting ready to break by the thump it makes each time it passes through the work. It's a bit unnerving when the blade finally goes with a bang, but it can do no harm, because when the blade does break, it will stop turning. The only precaution you need take is to keep your fingers well away from the blade.

Bandsaw blades eventually get dull, though, and filing one by hand, by putting it in a filing vise and taking a file to it, as you can do with hand and circular saw blades, is impossible. The temper of the teeth, which is so effective in giving a long-lasting sharpness, works against the filer. The tooth makes its toughness known the moment you run a file across it. The file does nothing in the way of sharpening but instead merely slips over the tooth, and the file itself is ruined.

I'm too stubborn and too tight to throw away an otherwise perfectly good saw blade, so I take it over to a fine abrasive cutting wheel—the kind you cut pipe with—and, holding it as close as I can to the proper angle of the tooth, thrust each tooth lightly against the wheel. Of course this is no proper way to sharpen a blade, but I find I can do it fast and do it a couple of times before I have to throw the blade away because the teeth have become too short and out of shape.

THE PORTABLE CIRCULAR SAW

The hand-held, portable circular saw, commonly referred to as a Skilsaw, was certainly a boon to the builder when it became available. Skilsaw is really a brand name, but the type is generally called "Skilsaw," even though many different manufacturers make them. It would be hard to say whether the house carpenter or the boatbuilder benefits most from them, but I for one am sure glad it was invented.

When a Skilsaw is used with a rip guide, it does the job of a tablesaw, and it can be tilted, the same as a tablesaw, from 0 to 45 degrees. A Skilsaw is especially good for a man working alone as I do, because I can't handle, say, a 4 x 8 sheet of plywood on my tablesaw without setting up a support of some kind for the sheet. I use my Skilsaw a lot in building the Instant Boats—sawing chines, gunwales, and large plywood shapes. To make sawing easier, whenever possible I put the pieces to be sawed on horses to avoid getting down on my hands and knees to do it. When I'm dealing with long, light pieces that won't stay put, I clamp them to the horses to saw them. Now that I think of it, that's probably why I attach so little importance to having a vise, unlike Lance Gunderson, who insisted you should build a vise before you build a boat.

I paid nearly $70 for my 6½-inch Porter Cable portable saw a little over 20 years ago, and it's still going strong. Today there are plenty of them on the market, some selling for as low as $20. The low-priced ones are cheaply made, with poor adjustments, such as wing nuts instead of a nice big knob to get a hold of, but I suppose they will do the job.

If you keep your mind on what you're doing, Skilsaws are no more dangerous to use than any other kind of power saw, but always remember this safety precaution: set the blade to a depth that will allow it to just come through the wood.

The earlier Skilsaws didn't have an automatic blade stop, so they coasted when the switch was off. This made them quite dangerous, especially if the saw guard happened to stick in the up position. A careless workman who sets a Skilsaw down on the floor with the blade still turning, and doesn't bother to check the guard, could find himself minus a toe or two for his moment of inattention. Injuries from this kind of carelessness are seldom heard of now. Today Skilsaws are made quite safe, even for dummies, with the blade stopping the moment the switch is released. Yet all isn't foolproof. Believe it or not, some people have actually felt the underside of the board to see if the saw was cutting through!

It's hard to say what brand of power tools is the best to buy anymore, because companies have bought out other companies and have changed their policies on tool quality. I do agree with Lance Gunderson, though, when he

65

says, "You can't trust any of the salesmen." I think if you really want to find out the best tool to buy or those not to buy, the best rule is: *just ask the man who uses one.*

7

The Best is None Too Good (Sometimes)

It didn't use to be that way . . . or, *Why don't they make them like they used to?* We hear both these themes quite often today, and they apply to a wide variety of the goods and services we buy. It would be nice to be able to put all the blame on the manufacturers for not making them "that way," but in my opinion, we have to accept at least part of the blame ourselves for becoming docile consumers. Over the years we have allowed ourselves to be victimized by the advertisers who prey on our seemingly inborn desire to keep up with the Joneses at all costs. How much of it springs from a conscious reaction, I don't know; I'm no psychiatrist. But I do see an acceptance of rather strange values by customers who drive into my yard to pick up a boat. They step out of a five- or six-thousand-dollar car that's maybe brand new, or close to it, that already shows rust spots under the shiny coat of paint, and they ask, as they are looking over a four- or five-hundred-dollar boat: "How long will it last?"

That never ceases to stagger me a little, since I know that a little, inexpensive boat will still be sailing, or could be if looked after, long after my questioner has driven three or four cars to the junkyard. You can't blame the customer for asking how long the boat will last, but I'll bet it's a question he never thinks of asking his car dealer.

I'm not suggesting that boats should be built like cars. Cars can be driven around with fenders falling off, with no great danger to the occupant—but boats can't drop a plank or two out in the middle of nowhere and expect to survive. I'm sure, however, that most boatbuilders are aware of the requirements.

GALVANIZED VS. BRONZE

Keeping a tray full of bronze nails around is expensive, but it isn't as bad for the full-time builder as it is for the one-shot amateur. The full-time builder buys an ample supply of nails of various sizes, knowing that he isn't likely to get stuck with a surplus just because he doesn't know exactly how many of what size he will use on a particular part of the hull. He simply uses the surplus next time. It's a different story if you're building only one boat. At six dollars a pound or so (at this writing, for bronze or copper nails), it's nice to come as close as you can to figuring how many you will need.

Four sizes of bronze nails fit the requirements for any of the Instant Boats. They are ⅞-inch, 1-inch, 1⅛-inch, and 1¼-inch number 13 wire nails, and you use them where their length suits best for holding power. A pound of each of these lengths is a good start for one of the Instant Boats. You can always buy more if you need them. Even that small amount is expensive enough, but to ask for less than a pound will probably get you a sour look from the supplier—who has maybe just sold a keg of them to the previous customer.

You'll need some copper nails as well, for fastening the side and bottom buttstraps where clenching is required. (To clench a nail is to drive it through the work and turn the point back into the wood.) Bronze nails are too brittle to clench. Screws could be used here instead of clenched nails, but they are even more expensive and much slower to drive.

Customers like the looks of bronze nails and fittings. Polished bronze oarlocks look very elegant sitting on a hull of matching finish, and I'll admit they make a good selling point. But for the Instant Boat builder, building only one for himself, I can't see using copper and bronze everywhere except for one reason: If you don't get a bronze nailhead sunk and filled properly, it still won't end up leaving a rust streak down the side of your boat, but a galvanized nail, with its head sanded because it was not properly countersunk, and with maybe only a thin coat of paint over it, will soon make itself known. Then again, galvanized fastenings are only about a tenth of the cost of bronze; you can realize quite a saving by going all the way with galvanized fastenings and fittings, including oarlocks, gudgeons, and pintles.

WHAT ABOUT CHEAPER WOODS?

If you want to cut costs even more, you might consider using a combination of galvanized fittings and AC plywood, or shop-grade plywood, which is even cheaper. For two years now I've been lugging around a sheet of ⅝-inch AC plywood, the type used in house construction, in the back of my pickup to protect the bottom of the box. I've never put anything on it in the way of a preservative, and it has been completely exposed to the elements, which in

Boat fittings, mostly bronze: oarlock with safety chain, side plate for oarlock, lap link, thimble, sailmaker's thimble, bow eye, eyebolt, cleat, snaphooks, gudgeon and pintle.

Maine include winters of alternate freezes and thaws. I never have a cap on my pickup, so sometimes there's a foot of snow on the plywood for a few weeks and next it will be floating in a pool of water from a sudden downpour, caused by clogged drainholes and a tight tailgate. I've thrown at least four or five cords of hard and heavy firewood onto the plywood, thereby giving it a dogeared appearance. It has also lain on the ground for infrequent intervals between use, but still it shows no signs of delamination.

I haven't built any boats from the cheapest grade of plywood yet, but it could help fill a need for a cheap skiff for a lobster fisherman. I speak from experience, having been a lobsterman. I've seen, and still see, how skiffs are rafted in a bunch, thrown on top of one another on a float, and even used as battering rams when launched, with the top one being slid over the one underneath. Unfortunately, it was not uncommon to go down to the wharf in the morning and find a hole punched in the side of your skiff, the center thwart hanging from one side, maybe with half or the whole transom missing because somebody with a to-hell-with-you-Bud attitude launched his skiff from atop yours. You can believe that in this case "buying cheap" is the first consideration. Don't knock it. Yet, if you go back to Chapter 3, you'll note that using a mixture of expensive and inexpensive materials is what helped drive up the cost of Lance Gunderson's Surf. If you want a cheap boat, you might as well go all the way as long as structural strength isn't jeopardized.

GOOD ENOUGH GLUES

Almost all glues on the market are good, and picking the right one appears to be more individual choice than anything else, as far as I can see. One man's favorite is often another man's failure. You pick yours and I'll pick mine.

I used Weldwood plastic resin glue for many years building small skiffs with mostly good results. The only failure that I recall happened once when the plywood came free from the oak stem and oak cheekpieces of the transom on one of these skiffs. Reflecting on that lone failure leads me to believe that part of the problem came from using green oak, together with the battering the boat took as a fisherman's skiff. Now I'm taking another look at Weldwood, since I've had the chance to see how it has held up over the years.

Just recently I got one of my old dories back; it was 10 years old and needed repair because of dry rot. Like the skiffs, I had built it with plywood and oak. It was one of six Gloucester Gull light dories built for Eugene Swan, owner of Pine Island Boy's Camp at Belgrade Lakes in Maine. It had seen plenty of hard service—you could tell that by the way the oarlocks wallowed around in the now paper-thin sockets, and from the heel prints worn through the top layers of the half-inch plywood bottom.

It's seldom that a builder gets a boat back after it leaves his shop, so he rarely has any way of knowing how his work and materials have held up. I always figured no news was good news and let it go at that, but this returned dory gave me an excellent chance to check up. I was delighted to find no signs of glue failure or fiberglass delamination. Dry rot is a common enough problem with boats used in fresh water for any length of time, so I felt no responsibility for that. I was much pleased to see her looking that good in view of the use she had received over the years.

I'll admit that I have had some doubts about this plastic water-mixed glue, partly because of much earlier, though dubious, failures, and partly from reading too much about glues. Articles and books pose such questions as: Is it gap-filling? How critical is temperature? How precise must the mixture be so as not to reduce bonding strength? These questions go on and on, and I think they tend to confuse the novice builder rather than help him.

One particularly asinine remark about the use of inexpensive plastic resin dry powder glue finally turned me off completely from the idea that any one type of glue is best for everyone to use. It went like this: "Plastic resin water-mixed glues can be used with good results above the waterline, but shouldn't be used below it, because a joint made with that kind of glue *won't stand boiling.*" (Italics mine.) I give Pete Culler credit for the shortest and best answer to that proposition in his book *Skiffs and Schooners*. Pete said: "If you're going to boil your boat, don't use it."

Seriously, I don't see any reason why this kind of glue shouldn't be used for building any of the Instant Boats, especially when no oak is involved. Oak-to-oak is a difficult joint for any glue to hold; I try to avoid depending on it. I prefer using plenty of fastenings with the glue to guarantee that such a joint will hold.

Plastic resin glue has a couple of other good features besides its cheapness. One is that the mixture is not critical. Plastic resin glue comes as a powder and is mixed with water; just mix it to a creamy consistency and go to it. The other good feature is that it's easy to clean any surplus glue from hands and brushes with just plain old water. I keep a bucket of water on my shop stove all the time, and use the warm water with a handy rag to wipe each joint after it has been glued and fastened.

Plastic resin glue is perfectly suitable as far as I know for the Instant Boat builder to start with. If you want to use more expensive types, go ahead. Buy the resorcinols or the epoxies, but brace yourself for the price.

PAINTS AND FILLERS

When customers come into my shop, often the first thing that catches their eye is a boat sitting there with a paint job they can see their faces in. I take pride in getting on a finish that good, but before you accuse me of breaking my arm to pat myself on the back, let me point out that it never used to be that way. I used to be just another painter until Gene Wiggin of Rockland, Maine, a professional housepainter and good friend, walked into my shop one day and caught me with a brush and a coffee can, trying to get a coat of paint on one of my dories.

He cleared his throat a couple of times and then said, "When are you going to throw that broom away and go buy yourself a decent brush?"

That rocked me a little. It would have upset me, coming from a stranger, but Gene was well known to me and so was his talent for putting on a coat of paint faster and better than anyone around. So I put my brush down and asked, "What do you mean?"

He told me. "Sounds like you're sweeping the floor with that dry brush. Why don't you put some *paint* on it, and *paint* with the paint . . . and while you're at it, get yourself a new brush. Look at the one you're using. It's all worn down, the bristles are too stiff, and there aren't enough of them to get a good brushful of paint on to start with, and even if there were, you keep wiping the brush off against the can instead of getting it on the boat."

I passed him the brush, "Okay, show me."

At once, Gene plunged my brush about a third of the way into the paint can and pulled it out loaded, and with absolutely no hesitation got it onto the side of the dory and started making long, smooth strokes.

I'll pass on Gene's advice to you. Get a charge of paint onto the surface and spread it out fast, with heavy enough pressure to spread it out evenly so it's neither too thick nor too thin, which will keep the paint from sagging. Load up your brush again, paint the bare area a foot or so ahead of the spot you've just done, and blend it back into the first area with the same pressure. Then for the final touch, use longer and lighter strokes all brushed in one direction to help flow the paint and give it that final mirror-like finish, free from any brush marks.

Gene was right, as he always is about paint, and now my boats look much the better for his advice.

Also at his suggestion, I bought half a dozen small metal paint pots. No more coffee cans, and no more growing a tired, paint-soaked thumb from hanging onto one. Paint pots get built up with layers of paint after a while and become quite heavy. The thing to do then is to set the pots outdoors in a safe open place, pour about a tablespoon of gasoline in each one, throw in a lighted piece of paper to touch them off, and stand clear. They will soon be clean, except for a small amount of crusty ash that can be cleaned out easily when cool with a putty knife and wire brush. Some painters shellac the inside of the cans before they use them again.

A word of caution here. I live in the country and can get away with stunts like that because no one is looking over my shoulder. If I lived in the city, I'd probably have second thoughts about touching off one of those paint pots and having it belch black smoke and stink into someone's open window—or some cop's car.

HOW TO BUY PAINT

Selecting the right kind of paint was a simple matter a few years ago. You simply asked for a can of paint of the color wanted, and if you happened on a good-natured clerk, he might even ask you how big a can and if you were going to use it inside or outside, if you had forgotten to tell him. For those who didn't want to bother even to be that selective, there was always a stack of "mill end" paint over in the corner that was something near a grey color and was cheap because it consisted of the leavings drained from a vat by the manufacturer before he had a new batch mixed. Back in the 1940s you could lug home a gallon of the stuff for a couple of bucks, and you can still buy it today for not much more than that. My experience with it years ago allows me to pass it by without any pangs, even if it is a bargain.

Almost all the paints in the not-too-distant past had one thing in common: they could be thinned with either turpentine or mineral spirits. If you felt a bit of the artist stirring in you, you could doctor up your paint a bit, with a slug of linseed oil if your brush was dragging in hot, dry weather, or a shot of Japan Drier if the day was cool and damp. You really didn't have to know a helluva lot. All you had to know was how to use a few ingredients that could be found in any hardware store, and if it looked like your day was going to be spoiled by the lack of one of them, chances were good you could borrow a little of it from a neighbor.

That's all changed today, and if you don't watch just what you're buying for paint, you could end up needing a degree in chemistry before daring to put a brush to your boat. Here's an example from my own experience, gained while I was painting the topsides of my powerboat on a warm summer's day. I'd started early in the morning as soon as the dew had dried, hoping to get it done before the sun got too high. I didn't make it. The sun climbed faster than I was stroking, the paint was becoming draggier by the minute, and it was starting to show overlaps. Of course, when I bought the paint I neglected to ask for any kind of thinner, and the salesman hadn't bothered to ask me if I wanted any, so I guess it was my fault for being caught short. Anyway, I read the directions— admittedly, a little late—and found the following: "Use our brand of Number 111 drying retarder." The label went on to warn that using anything other than their own Number 111 could ruin the job.

Well, only God and the manufacturer knew what the formula was for good old Number 111, and neither one was telling, so I jumped into my pickup and drove eight miles to Rockland to pick up the stuff, drove eight miles back, and finished the job. You can safely bet that now whenever I buy paint, I read the directions in the store, to see if it can be used with the ingredients I'm used to.

TWO OF EACH COAT WILL DO THE JOB

Let's get right down to the bare wood. Some builders have trouble getting a good paint finish on plywood "because of the grain"—or so they say. I'm not sure what the basis for their excuse is, but I strongly suspect that the quality of some paint jobs that need excuses reflects just how much work the builder has *not* put into them. Take a good look at the plywood surface before you start painting. If it shows water stains, look for raised grain, and sand lightly to get all dust and dirt off *before* attempting to paint.

Do all the fiberglassing first, including sanding it, before doing any sealing and painting. The painting method I use is my own and it works. I'll tell you the kinds of paints and sealers I use, in case you want to use them, but almost any of the paints on the market today will do the job nicely—and that includes the ones with the fancy driers, too. The important thing is to stick to one brand as much as possible, learning its secrets and buying only the additives that are compatible with it.

Sealing the grain comes first. I use Weldwood Deep Finish Firzite, a thin, resinous type, applying two coats of it, one right after the other, paying particular attention to working it into the edge grain. Allow this sealer to dry overnight before you apply any paint over it. If your shop is cold, say 45 degrees or thereabouts, put a shot of Japan Drier in the sealer. That will set it up.

Next come the two undercoats. They should be put on quite thick, because they are intended to fill small crevices and slight imperfections in the wood. These are the coats that are sanded and filled very carefully, because they are the base for the final two finish coats (like the foundation cream for a woman's face—well, *some* women's faces). Any imperfections left on the last layer of the undercoat will show right through to the final finish coat; this will happen, believe it or not, even when more than two finish coats are used.

I use a neutral base undercoat made by Baltimore Paint Company. Neutral base means no color, and I choose it because you can tint it by dumping some of the finish coat in (amount not critical). This means your boat will stay the same color even if some finish paint gets knocked off her.

I almost always put a little drier in the undercoat, unless the weather is really hot and dry. Undercoaters have a good deal of oil in them, and I want their dried surfaces to be hard enough to stand power sanding without clogging the 100-grit sandpaper. If the paint dries to a good, hard surface, both the paint dust and the surface itself will have a chalky look, which makes it easy to spot the darker-colored depressions caused by hammer blows, and any other imperfections missed by the sanding process.

You can fill the holes in the wood surface with any auto body filler—no special choice, as far as I'm concerned. All the ones I've seen are mixed with a colored cream hardener that comes in a tube. Mixing it isn't critical; all it takes is about a quarter-inch length of hardener to set up a batch of filler about the size of a golf ball, which is enough to mix up at a time for most small dents and nail holes. If you mix more, quite likely you'll have to throw out part of it, because the stuff sets up even more quickly than polyester resin.

Sand the filled places once they've set up, and then give the hull a second coat of undercoater. Sand the whole hull again after that has dried. Check again for missed spots and hairline cracks, and fill any you find with Woolsey or International trowel cement—a very soft and easy-to-apply white putty that does a nice job of obliterating minor imperfections.

Trowel cement is slow-drying, though, so don't expect to be able to paint your boat right off, as you can when using auto body fillers. If you're in a hurry, you can use auto body filler if you thin it sufficiently with polyester resin so it will go into cracks.

With the two base coats on (more, if needed to get a good base), you're ready for the final finish coats of gloss or whatever your choice might be. I use Woolsey Yacht Paints mostly, and I prefer the semi-gloss to the full-gloss for its softer look. In fact, I really like a flat finish, and I'd use it on my own boats except that it shows scuff marks and dirt too soon.

I always thin the final coats a little, and take pains to brush them out well to avoid any sags. No matter how careful you are, sags still form easily on a vertical surface, and you have to watch for them constantly. That's why it's a good idea to keep looking back over the area you've just painted, trying to spot those drips. Sags and missed spots are best seen by looking along the length of the hull, rather than broad on. So stop every so often and check for them—brush the sags out and cover the dry areas before the paint sets up. On a cold day I warm the paint a little, rather than keep on adding thinner, to make it flow on properly.

Dark colors always take longer to dry than light ones, so they need a healthier slug of drier. I dislike using dark colors for that reason and another—they invariably show dust and any imperfection that might have been missed while applying the undercoaters, much more so than lighter colors do.

TOUCH-UP JOBS

I often wonder how the phrase "touch-up job" ever got started. I always thought touch-up meant that, if you spotted a booboo after your paint job had thoroughly dried, you could just sand the area lightly, throw on another scant brushful of the same paint, and not see any sign of tinkering at all. Not so for me. When I tried touching up a spot, say, right in the middle of the side of a dory, the result looked so awful I had to paint the whole outside of the hull all over again.

I learned one thing from my touch-up experiences, though, even if I learned the lesson the hard way, and that was not to put the final coats on the outside of the hull until the seats were fastened to the risers. I used to paint my dories inside and out first and put the varnished seats in last, until one day a screw I was driving to hold the seat ran into one of the anchor nails used to fasten the seat riser. The screw backed the nail right out through my nice paint job, *and through the outside of the hull,* all proud and clear. The first time it happened, I chalked it up to bad luck. When it happened the second time, I figured that luck was no longer a valid excuse. So I made that slight change in the finishing sequence, preferring to do that rather than to paint the entire hull all over again for one little nailhead.

A PAINT-SAVING TIP THAT WORKS

For years, throwing away unused paint that had hardened in the can bothered me. To keep paint fresh, among other things I'd tried a dragon's breath of cigar smoke, blown into the paint can off the top of a freshly eaten horseradish sandwich. I had hopes of dispelling the oxygen just as I quickly slammed the cover on. Nothing seemed to work.

It wasn't until 1973 when the energy thing happened and drove up the price of everything, including paint, that I got serious and decided I didn't want to throw away any more paint. Previously, small amounts of paint left in a gallon can, especially in the summer, would end up being thrown out. If any of the paint could be used at all, it would take me longer to break up the crust and strain it out of the paint than it was worth.

It often pays to keep an eye on your wife, especially in the kitchen, where she has developed her own techniques and expertise just as the builder does in his shop. Watching Amy put a piece of waxed paper on a freshly baked chocolate pie to keep it from skimming over gave me the solution to the half-used-can-of-paint problem. If that waxed paper kept the air off chocolate pie, it ought to keep the air off paint, too. The next thing was to figure out the easiest way to cut the paper just the right size so it would float down inside the can—it had to be neither too loose nor too tight. I soon found that the can cover, placed upside down on the waxed paper, makes exactly the right pattern for a nearly perfect fit. Just hold the cover down with one hand and trim around it with a knife point. The paper disc will float on the paint's surface and effectively block out all air.

I cut a bunch of waxed-paper discs ahead of time and keep a supply handy. I always plop one into the can, even if I'm going to use the paint the next day, knowing it will prevent skimming over and save me the trouble of straining it. The waxed-paper disc will stick to the sides of the can after long storage, just from the hairline crack between its edge and the can, but that still causes no trouble or mess. Just gently tap all around the edge of the paper to break it free, toss it away, and replace it with a fresh one. It's something of a nuisance to spend the time cutting those discs out, but straining paint is a much bigger nuisance, and knowing that I don't have to throw paint out makes all the trouble worthwhile.

CHOOSE YOUR WEAPONS

Selecting the paint brush—the best size and the type of bristle—is important and deserves considerable thought, though I'll admit I didn't do much thinking about it myself until Gene Wiggin brought it to my attention. Soon after he accused me of painting with a broom, I bought the best badger-hair brushes I could find. The prices rocked me a little, but I paid up and brought the brushes home, and I've been using them ever since.

It's good to have brushes in several sizes—the smaller ones for getting into corners and other hard-to-reach places inside the hull, the larger ones on the

Painting supplies: turpentine, paint bucket, Japan Drier, putty knives, badger-hair brushes.

outside where nothing is in the way. My choices are 1½-inch, 2½-inch, and 3-inch brushes.

You can identify the badger-hair brush by the dark stripe that runs across the white bristles. What makes them so expensive, of course, is that these stiffer bristles are found only on European and Asiatic badgers; American badger hair is too soft for any but decorative purposes. At any rate, these imported badger-hair brushes will suck up a brushful of paint and lay it on better than any others I've used.

Along with your good brushes, you will also need some bum ones. You should have an ample supply of throwaways for use with glue and resin, and on any job where conditions will damage the bristles. Rough jobs are all the nylon-bristle types are good for, anyway, and they usually have to be thrown out after the first use—any kind of use. Nylon brushes are too limber for glue, and I don't care for them for painting, either. Unfortunately, they seem to be the only cheap brushes you can buy today.

But here's a domestic exception. Back in 1974 I saw an advertisement by a Southern manufacturer who was offering small, throwaway pure-bristle brushes (source unspecified; I suspected hog). Maybe because I appreciate honesty in advertising and get so little opportunity to respond to it, I sent off an order for three dozen and got my boxful right back.

Here's the kicker. I'm still using them, and they are so good I can't see throwing them away; they get cleaned right along with Europe's best. Apparently my wife recognizes value, too, because she swiped two of them for pastry brushes. The only supplier I know of is the Glovers Mills Company, P. O. Box 4888, Hialeah, Florida 33014. If you can get any, latch onto them, and you'd better hoard them.

PAMPER YOUR PAINT BRUSHES

You should clean a paint brush right after each use. Never leave it standing on its bristles for any length of time, and don't dump it into thinner with only half the bristles immersed. Gasoline cleans bristles best; it's also fastest and cheapest. But I don't recommend using the resulting soup for lighting your woodstove fire. To get rid of it, throw it on an old board or on your shop steps—they're always paint-thirsty.

Overnight soaking in paint remover will work well for brushes hardened a little by paint, but there is some risk of the fumes attacking your lungs or a splatter of solvent burning your eye. It seems the price of having a super-clean brush is a choice between getting blown up or being poisoned. Maybe that explains why you see so many dirty and neglected brushes lying around.

I've named specific types and brands here. I stand by my choices, more especially by my techniques, but with all the new products on the market and new ones coming along all the time, I wouldn't want to pick the best from among all of them. The ones I mention work best for me for what I build. But choosing materials depends to a great extent on the degree of quality that you as a builder want to put into your boat.

So in the end it boils down pretty much to personal preference.

8

The Pleasures of a Simple Rig

Start simple and start early—that is the best way to learn to sail. But do it in a boat, instead of the way I began some 40 years ago—on dry land and in a four-wheeled homemade cart with a bedsheet for a sail.

My childhood chum Lee Wotton and I waited for a good windy day and hoisted sail in the middle of his driveway. With Lee pushing (he was bigger) and me steering by foot control, we got her flying over the driveway. I was experiencing my first, free, wind-driven ride. This moment of bliss was short-lived, however, for a sudden blast of wind sent me across Lee's lawn, out of control, and headed for an open sink drain, which was a type of sewer commonly found in many country homes before the days of indoor plumbing. It consisted simply of a pipe leading directly from the sink through the side of the house and into a trough run out on the lawn, where everything that was poured down the sink gathered into a sludge pool.

That's where I was headed, and there was no avoiding it. The front wheels fell in, stopping me short and pitching me head first into the stinking mess. All open sewers have the same odor; if you have smelled one, you have smelled them all. Luckily, Lee's mother, Beulah, took heart and cleaned most of the guck off me and then sent me home, where my mother finished the job.

By way of comparison, Roger Taylor's account of how he learned to sail (told in his book *Good Boats*, International Marine Publishing Company, Camden, Maine) has much more appeal, at least from the environmental aspect. Roger, then seven, was not enthusiastic about being cast adrift in a flat-bottomed, narrow-beamed contraption with square ends made by his father, who told him: "This is the day you learn to sail." Roger started off anyway, without benefit of either leeboard or rudder. His father told him to steer by shifting his weight to keep one side immersed, and to tack her by walking around the mast and quickly moving aft again.

I have never heard of anyone learning to sail that way before, but I can't imagine a better one. The rig was about as simple as they come, but the tricky part, as usual, was learning what to do with what you had. In Roger's case, the learning was achieved with the help of a good teacher plus his own determination to see it through. Few of us are lucky enough to start sailing so young, with so good a teacher. To me, what seemed most important about the experience was that Roger learned to do it first the hard way. After that, it must have been a piece of cake for him when he was allowed to use a rudder and leeboard.

About 10 years passed before I tried sailing again. I probably wouldn't have bothered except that a small wherry I had bought to lobster-fish with around Metinic Island came equipped with a spritsail and a centerboard.

Attempts at sailing the wherry proved futile as far as getting her to windward was concerned. The only successful run I ever made was on a broad reach covering the five miles from Metinic to Spruce Head in a little over an hour and a half—not exactly a sleigh ride, but the warmth of the sun, a steady southwest breeze, and a portable radio made the day a memorable one for me. She was going where she was pointed, and there were no sink drains in sight.

I gave up sailing after that, partly because I preferred to remember one good sail rather than a bunch of poor ones, in case I should get interested again, and partly because I turned to power, which I would stick to for the rest of my fishing career.

I'll never know why I couldn't get that wherry to go to windward, but at the time I didn't particularly care, because the days of hauling lobster pots by sail-driven craft were over long before my time. What did impress me, though, was the simplicity of the spritsail.

Getting the rig set up was easy. It took only a minute or two to unfurl the sail, plop the mast in the hole through the forward thwart, and step it. The peak of the sail had a pigtail with an overhand knot in it. You caught the pigtail with the tapered slotted end of the sprit and shoved the peak of the sail up hard. The rounded heel of the sprit was caught in an eyesplice in a piece of rope about three or four feet long. This rope led through a thimble spliced into a sling hung on the mast, and from the thimble down to a cleat. All it took to peak the sail was a push up on the sprit heel and a pull down on the line running to the cleat to which you secured the line.

You could get the sail off her in a hurry just by releasing the line from the cleat, and down it would come. You stowed the rig quickly by freeing the sprit, pulling the mast out of the step, furling the sail against the mast, and wrapping up the whole thing with the sheet.

The other good feature of the sprit rig was that it was very forgiving of beginners. With the sprit carried high on the loose-footed sail, it was impossible to get a crack aside the head in a sudden jibe. Should the captain feel his craft was being overpowered by a sudden gust on a downwind run, he could easily spill the wind by slacking the sheet and letting the sail trail out over the bow. There were no stays in the way, and the mast could rotate freely—so let her go.

After the little sailing experience I had around 1946, I never set foot in a sailboat again until years later, convinced that the art of sailing was a mysterious thing that other people practiced. I was too busy catching lobsters and chasing women to learn, so I paid no further attention to it.

That was all to change, though, in 1970, when I started selling boat plans and asked Phil Bolger to design a small daysailer for me. The requirements were simple (or so I thought). All I wanted was a boat that could be used to take advantage of whatever the day might bring for weather. Oars for rowing if the wind pooped out (I'd seen plenty of sailboats sitting around in a calm with no provision for rowing), a sail if the owner felt like sailing, and a small motor if he strayed farther than he wanted to row or was faced with a long beat home. In other words, I wanted a boat that could do it all. I didn't bother to tell Phil what I thought the boat should look like, thinking I'd asked for enough already. I did mention, though, that I had tried the sprit rig and had a liking for it.

There was a long waiting period until the plans arrived, or so it seemed, because Phil is always prompt. They finally did arrive, along with the explanation that Phil had fallen into bed with some kind of vile virus. My wife Amy got the first look at them, because I was out hauling my lobster traps, so she beat me to the mailbox. She called on the CB radio to say the plans had arrived and tried to explain without much success what the boat looked like, finally saying, "Wait 'til you see it. He must have been really sick!"

Amy's not-so-subtle warning about the boat's appearance didn't jar me much, because I had already seen some of Phil's other unusual designs. That he doesn't design the same boat over and over again is one of the things that attracted me to his designing in the first place.

So it was with only a slight amount of apprehension that I looked at the pointy-nosed, high-chined, V-bottomed boat with a wide stern that Phil called the Thomaston Galley. For sure I'd never seen anything like it, but perhaps to soften the blow, Phil drew her with a spritsail rig, which was the only feature that did look familiar.

Building the Thomaston Galley took all the skills that the builder of Instant Boats doesn't need, such as lofting, making a jig, handling changing bevels, and a number of other refinements. The boat was worth the effort, though, and when she was ready for the water, it was up to me to get her sailing. I hadn't

The Thomaston Galley in a fresh breeze off Spruce Head, Maine. (Photo by Wilma Huntley)

tried sailing since 1946, and now, 24 years later, I found myself striking out in a gusty nor'wester in a strange new boat. The difference this time was that I expected it to sail because Phil Bolger said it would, unlike the wherry, whose design was totally by guess and by God. *And sail it did!*

The first attempt proved quite awkward. At times the boat was laid down to the gunwale in a gust, then she gathered speed, only to lose it again just at the moment of coming about, which caused her to stop and back up—a bit unsettling. That sail seemed worth recording with a movie camera, so now we sit in our living room and look back on it. Viewing that experience now shows a poorly peaked sail, too much wind, and a poor sailor, all reminding me of a duck trying to fly with a broken wing.

I've had to learn to sail right along with the builders I've sold plans to, and it has been fun. One of the things that learning to sail has taught me is that powerboat experience gives little head start toward learning to sail. Not realizing that you don't tie up a sailboat as you do a powerboat, and then forget about it, gave me a moment of anxiety and embarrassment one day when I was sailing the Galley.

I had tired of sailing that warm, sunny afternoon and decided to tie up to something looking like a thin metal fence stake sticking up out of water in a sheltered cove on the lee side of Spruce Head Island. Thinking only how nice it was going to be to stretch out in the sun, I sailed the Galley up to the stake, luffed her, and tied the end of the sheet to the stake, leaving the rudder and leeboard in place. I walked back aft and settled down on the cockpit sole with my back propped against the aft bulkhead and watched with detached interest the ever-increasing distance between the boat and the stake as the sheet and sail trailed out over the bow.

I watched through half-closed eyes as she drifted back, taking the slack out of the sheet and sail, finally bringing up on the stake, which was now about 30 feet from where I was sitting. Thinking all was well, I settled back, concerned only with finding the best position, when I felt the Galley move off sideways and gather speed. Instantly alerted, but with a feeling of stunned incomprehension, I braced myself with both hands and watched the sail fill. The end of the sheet was out of my grasp, still tied to the stake.

The Galley weighs only 135 pounds and is a bit tender with only one aboard, so I had second thoughts about trying to stand up and make a grab for anything while she was in motion. I knew that my added weight up by the mast wasn't going to help a bit when she fetched up, so I resisted the urge to try to do anything until she did what she was going to do.

She wasn't long in reaching the end of the scope she had, and when she did, the bow went down and she rolled her side down, but with a rather springy feeling. Nothing snapped or parted, so when she popped up again, I dashed forward, grabbed the foot of the sail, and worked my way back to the stake. I grabbed the end of the sheet, much relieved that I didn't get my butt soaked or break anything from my stupid mistake. A quick look around showed that no one was watching, so, with silent thanks to whatever deity looks after hapless sailors, I cast off and chalked up that experience as the price paid for learning something by yourself.

THE LEEBOARD

Getting used to the leeboard took a while. At first, the looks of it bothered my purist instincts when I saw it on the Galley. Like almost everyone else, I thought any respectable boat should have a centerboard. I suppose the only

83

reason I felt that way was that all the boats I'd seen around these parts had one. That wasn't much of an excuse to have doubts about the leeboard, but it was the only one I had, so my prejudice was built around it.

Seldom do I ever ask Phil why he designed something a certain way, preferring to find out for myself under trial. I figured he probably had many good reasons for sticking a leeboard on the Galley, and all the Instant Boats, too, but to me—except for the extra room gained from not having a center-board—those reasons didn't become apparent until later on after I used leeboards for a time and came to understand how they worked.

One thing I wondered about, as have others, is the placement of the board. Don't you have to swap sides with the leeboard every time you change tacks? The answer is no. Sure, there is strain on the board when it is left on the weather side, but I've yet to break one. Even if the board does break sometime, the job of building another to replace it will be less trouble than the constant bother of shifting it on each tack.

The leeboard has other advantages, too. For one thing, it doesn't spoil the rowing qualities of the boat, as does a centerboard with its necessary hole through the boat's bottom. But the feature I like best about the leeboard is that it's always right where it can be seen and reached. Here in Maine there is a lot of floating seaweed, eelgrass, and lobster buoys to foul things up, so it's nice to be able to reach down and clear off the mess and keep on sailing.

A few years ago I managed to stop a leak in an old centerboard sloop, one that was regularly filling overnight, by running some fiberglass up into the case. That took care of the leak for about four years, but the old boat works all the time, and of course the case is now leaking again.

Last summer a small, beautifully finished sailboat was left in my yard by the owner for me to resell. A young lady came along and bought it, used it once or twice, and brought it back a few days later, saying, "It's the centerboard. It's stuck and won't go up or down." By this time I'd been using leeboards long enough so that all I could offer was sympathy. As far as I know, the board is still stuck. I don't have much patience with things that are pretty but won't work.

Sometimes it takes a while to understand why Phil designs things as he does, but finding out is usually just a matter of using what he's come up with, and letting time and experience provide the answer.

Of the two types of spritsails—the type used on the Galley and that used on the Instant Boats—I have a slight preference for the latter, mainly for the ease of setting it and also of striking it when the wind blows up. I like the looks of the Galley sail better, but trying to catch the small pigtail in the slot of the sprit often takes more than just a few tries when the sail is whipping around. Also, the foot of the Galley's sail is carried so low that it makes seeing where you're going difficult. I am always lifting the foot of the Galley's sail to see where I am headed.

The triangular-shaped spritsail of the Instant Boats is set in the same way as the Galley's sail. The only difference is that the sprit slot is caught in the sheet where it is attached to the clew, which makes the sprit end much easier to reach when the wind is blowing. There doesn't seem to be any difference in power between the two rigs, so for the extra convenience of the triangular sail, I'd just as soon stick to it. The foot of the Instant Boat sail is higher up from the mast partner than the Galley's, and the cut of the sail allows the sprit boom to be placed high enough so that you don't have difficulty seeing where you are going. Yet you still have the safety advantage of having a loose-footed sail.

To attach one of these sails to the mast is easy enough; all that is required is a piece of nylon line, number 300 or heavier. The kind of line used for knitting lobster pot heads is plenty good enough, though I would choose the braided type because it doesn't unravel as the laid type does. Just bore a small hole athwartships in the mast about an inch from the top and attach the first grommet at the head of the sail to it, then tie each grommet individually after that with the nylon line. All that's needed is one turn through the grommet and around the mast; tie it off with a square knot backed with two overhand knots to avoid any chance of the knot slipping (nylon is slippery). If you have a rope-cutting heat gun, it's a good idea to melt the nylon ends right down onto the overhand knots.

Backing a knot with another knot like that reminds me of a TV show that had contestants trying to tie up an escape artist with what looked like at least four or five fathoms of rope. They could tie him up any way they wanted but had to do it within a prescribed time limit. Boy Scouts, firemen, and one navyman all tried to immobilize the victim. If the fellow wasn't loose by the end of the show, the contestant would lug away some money.

Not one was successful, and to a fisherman the reason was obvious. The lengthy piece of rope was the victim's gimmick. No one thought to back any of the knots, and it would have been difficult anyway with that much rope. The contestants just used the excess rope to wrap him up like a mummy, hoping it would hold. Even though the victim looked securely trussed, he only needed to shake himself a few times to be free.

I got quite involved watching the show, even to the point of taking them up on their offer to fly anyone from any part of the country to have a crack at tying up their escape artist. Those who know me would agree that I must have been quite sure I could do it, because it takes quite a lot to get me out of the state of Maine.

Anyway, they didn't pick me, which came as a great relief. I did hope they would make the mistake of picking a fisherman, one who depended on secure knots for putting bread on the table, and I was absolutely delighted one night when they announced that a man from Maine—a crewman on a sardine carrier—was going to give it a try.

I sat right on the edge of my chair watching with delight as the fisherman, using just a short length of the rope, tied the fellow's wrists quickly behind his back, then coiled the rest of the rope up and used the coil to tie a couple of backing knots against the knots already tied. One more knot was tied around the victim's ankles, and that was backed up, too. All done, the challenger threw the rest of the coil on the floor and went back into the audience to await the results.

At the end of the show the escape artist was twisting and turning, sweating profusely, and hadn't yet started a knot. The sponsor paid up, and that was the end of that gimmick.

ZEPHYR'S MEDITERRANEAN RIG

Like the Thomaston Galley and her Instant Boat sister ships, Zephyr's rig is very simple with nary a frill. At 20 feet 9 inches length overall, Zephyr has a long and lean look that goes well with her rakish lateen sail. The stubby 9-foot mast is made round and is free to revolve in its step. There is only a smooth hole at the truck for the halyard. The halyard is made fast to the yard, which is nothing but a 16-foot by 1½-inch slice off a two by four. The yard is held against the mast by a loose-fitting cringle (a piece of rope formed into a circle), and it slides up and down the mast controlled by the halyard, which runs to a cleat on the mast just above the mast partner on the side away from the sail. The boom, too, is square in cross-section, and the sheet is spliced around the boom through a couple of wooden cleats that act as stops. The sail is attached to both yard and boom by separate ties, just as with the sprit rig. A tack rope is led through a hole in the forward part of the boom and knotted, and from there it leads around the mast and back to a cleat on the boom, with enough length to let the boom go forward when the sail is reefed.

I like the lateen rig, finding it just as easy to handle as the spritsail. One feature I particularly like is that when you drop the sail, the yard and boom come down in a hurry and land down low, where it's easy to grab the sail and furl it.

It doesn't matter to me which rig I'm using, as long as I get there and back. They all work well, because they're well balanced. I find myself sailing with no hands on the tiller a lot of days when the wind is reasonably steady. Just working the sheet a little and shifting your weight is all that's needed. Sometimes when the wind is light, I like to put the tiller hard over and leave it there, letting the boat go around and around in her own length. All the Instant Boats will do this—the Punt best of all, I suppose because of her short length, absence of a keel, and a lot of bottom rocker.

For those of you who wonder at my being so easily entertained, I'll say only that I look on it as a virtue for making the long Maine winters bearable.

A good deal of credit for the Instant Boats' sailing capabilities belongs to the expertise of E.S. Bohndell and Son, Rockport, Maine, sailmakers since the early 1930s. Let me tell you why.

As I said before, my prime concern with sailing is that the rig be able to get me out and get me back, so I paid little attention to how effective proper sail cutting could be until I sold the first sail I had for the Galley and had to buy another. A friend of mine, lobster-buyer Nate Peasley, wanted the original sail to stick on an old peapod, so I sold it to him and bought my new one from Henry Bohndell. (The original sail had been made by an awning company.) What a difference in both looks and windward performance! I was delighted with it. My immediate reaction was, "Wow, this is the difference between a Model-T Ford and a Cadillac."

I've never tried making a sail and don't intend to, so for those who buy plans and later ask how to make the sail, I can't offer much help, other than to tell them that International Marine Publishing Company in Camden, Maine, sells books on how to make your own sails. For would-be sailmakers, that could be a good place to look for practical, usable advice.

After experiencing firsthand the difference between those two sails—one made by an awning-maker and the other by a professional sailmaker—I'm quite convinced that the sailmaker fully complements the designer in achieving first-rate performance.

Not much can go wrong with any of the rigs Phil Bolger has designed, so the inventory of spare parts to carry is simple, too. All I take with me in the Zephyr is a pair of oars, a bailing dish, life preservers, and a short length of nylon twine for use as a lashing in case of a failure.

RIGGING THE FOLDING SCHOONER

If I had followed my first impulse on seeing the Folding Schooner's sail plan, I would never have built her. Shown fully rigged and ready to sail, she was a bit overwhelming. Entirely unfamiliar with the details of the schooner rig as I was, my reaction was simply, "I can't do it." My problem was that I was trying to take her all in at once—a prime example of the futility of trying to absorb everything that the eye sees at one time. At first I wasn't able to see her basic simplicity.

The rig doesn't call for much hardware. Only two blocks are needed, one each for the fore and main sheets. The running rigging—her throat and peak halyards—lead through holes in the masts and are belayed to conveniently located pins.

For the novice, the difficulty of rigging the Folding Schooner comes from ignorance of the terminology used to describe various elements and functions. It was all new to me when I first unrolled Phil's blueprints. But his number system of labeling saved the day, and my lack of familiarity with the details of the rig didn't turn out to be much of a handicap after all.

Take just one detail—that piece of line attached to the after end of the main gaff and running through the uppermost hole at the masthead. It is called the peak halyard. I'd never have known its name, since I had no experience with the various parts of a schooner's rigging, but with Phil's plans, being able to read was all it took. A number 71 drawn inside a circle sat right on that piece of gear, and in the detailed instructions, number 71 told me it was a peak halyard. In the numbered building sequence plan key, number 71 identifies fore and main throat and peak halyards, and the main staysail halyard—all ¼-inch Dacron, running through well-faired ¾-inch-diameter holes cut through the mastheads as shown. So that wasn't hard, even though I didn't know one thing about it before I studied the plans. There is one requirement in using this sytem, however, and it is simply that the builder must follow directions exactly and not go wandering off on his own.

To go on. The rigging job I worried most about was boring the holes for the running rigging of the Folding Schooner's foremast. The sail plan shows five pieces of rigging, each doing a different job, and calls for six holes to be bored through the finished mast within a space of about two feet. At that, it would be no big deal if you did bore a hole in the wrong place. A wooden plug could be glued in the hole to take care of that kind of mistake. But especially when you don't know anything about an operation, it's fun to see if you can do it right the first time. What made the job difficult for me was that the holes had to be bored through the mast in different directions and at different angles according to the function of each particular piece of running rigging. The plans plainly show both profile and fore-and-aft views of the mast, but don't say which view you are looking at. Of course, anyone the least bit knowledgeable on the subject wouldn't have much trouble understanding which view they were seeing. But for me it meant studying each piece of rigging to find out what it was called, where it led, and what its function was before I bored a hole for it.

What I am saying is that there is too much there for the novice to understand all at one time, but trying to do that is all too typical of many amateur builders. It is probably one of the main reasons lots of boats never get built.

Don't allow yourself to be overwhelmed by a plan by trying to grasp it all at once. Take one thing at a time and follow it through. Before you know it, the whole thing will fit together in a completely understandable (and fully understood) picture. The sail plan that once seemed impossible to decode has given up its secrets without your being aware of it. The proof comes when you pick up the plan once more and see that what was once mysterious now has meaning. That's your reward.

The moral is that all the Instant Boats are simple, even the Folding Schooner, if you take each one of them step by step.

9

Building Teal Step by Step

When Phil Bolger designed the 12-foot Teal, the end result, he remarked with his usual self-disparaging modesty, "is the prettiest two sheets of plywood I've ever seen." I agree, but the really impressive thing is how those two sheets of plywood are put together to look that good. That's what we will see as we build the Teal, step-by-step, in this chapter.

Karin Knudsen, Assistant to the Publisher of the *National Fisherman*, wanted to build a small sailboat, so I happily accepted her volunteered services as model and tyro builder to help me record the process of building the Teal. This was Karin's very first boatbuilding attempt, and she faced it head-on. What little woodworking she had done in the past was limited to small jobs around the house using a few simple hand tools. In the course of building the Teal, she learned to use all the power tools in my shop, getting accustomed to them a little timidly at first but with increasing confidence as the building went on.

That's getting a little ahead of the story, so let's describe the process in a numbered building sequence—the same one that appears on the Teal plans in a condensed form. It is definitely worthwhile to elaborate on each step a little more thoroughly here, because the techniques of building the Teal are basic to building all the other Instant Boats. Any differences you will meet on the other boats will be very slight.

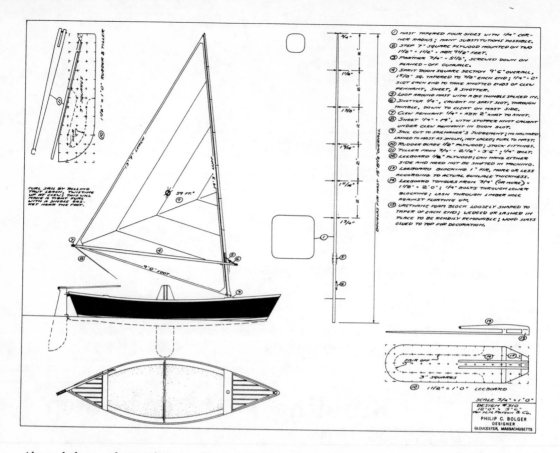

Above, below, and opposite, top: *Plans and instructions for building the Instant Boat Teal. Design by Phil Bolger for Harold Payson.*

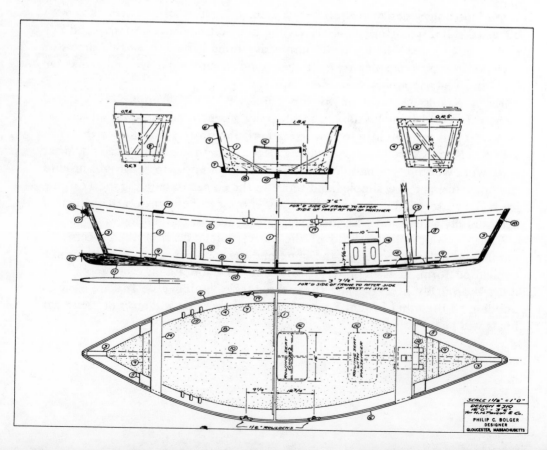

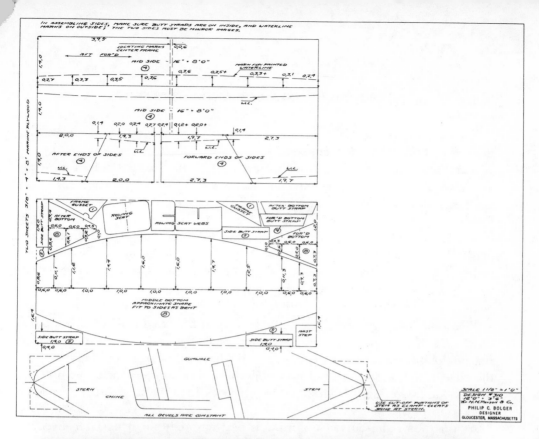

IN ASSEMBLING SIDES, MAKE SURE BUTT STRAPS ARE ON INSIDE, AND WATERLINE MARKS ON OUTSIDE; THE TWO SIDES MUST BE MIRROR IMAGES.

SCALE 1 1/2" = 1' 0"
DESIGN #310
12' 0" - 3' 6"
for H. H. Payson & Co.
PHILIP C. BOLGER
DESIGNER
GLOUCESTER, MASSACHUSETTS

Preparing to build her own Teal, Karin Knudsen studies the plans and instruction sheets.

STEP 1: SIDE ASSEMBLY AND BUTTSTRAPS

This is going to look like one hell of a long step, but only because not one move you'll make has been omitted.

Start by making the sides from a piece of ⅜-inch, 4-foot by 8-foot plywood as shown on the plywood layout plan at the top left corner. Two-thirds of the sheet are used to make the midsides, and the other third is used to make the forward and after pieces of the sides. Note the measurements 1, 4, 0 − 1, 4, 0 − 1, 4, 0, which indicate you are to cut the sheet into three straight rectangular panels 16 inches wide and 8 feet long. (If you've already forgotten about "feet, inches, eighths," go back and re-read Chapter 4.) Just hook your steel pocket rule on the side of the plywood at the end of the sheet and place a mark at 16 inches and 32 inches. Go to the other end and repeat the measurement.

Now take a straightedge long enough to span the length of the sheet, put it on the 16-inch marks, and draw a straight line the entire length of the sheet. Repeat for the 32-inch marks. If you don't have a straightedge handy, just use the edge of the second sheet of plywood you will be using to make the bottom. Simple—just two straight lines, and you have divided the sheet into three equal parts to form the boat's sides.

At this point the curved waterline is best ignored; put it on later after the sides have been made full length, when you can do it easily all in one crack. For now, let's stay with straight lines, two of which we have already drawn on the plywood.

Next locate the position of the center frame on the two midsides. Mark off 3, 9, 5 from the left end of the plywood sheet on one edge. Do it again from the same end, but on the other edge, and connect the two marks with a straightedge. Put another line ¾ inch away and parallel to that, and your center frame is located.

Squaring the line that way by using the plywood sheet as a big square is faster, easier, and more accurate than using a 2-foot framing square, which has a tendency to go askew from ragged edges and glue buildups.

We can now lay out the forward and after ends of the sides, which are shown on the bottom of the plywood sheet, right under the midsides, and mark them for cutting. To ensure that they get properly located, write "aft" and "forward" on the ends of the midsides.

That completes the laying out of the sides. They are ready now for cutting. Place the sheet of plywood on sawhorses or on the floor with spacers under the sheet to protect the floor or horses from being sawed when the sheet is cut. Put a planer blade in the Skilsaw and adjust it so it just goes through the plywood. Go to it, splitting the line for each cut. You must split the line in order to make the three panels of equal width. Leaving the line would make one piece a saw-cut short of 16 inches.

Place the cut sides on a flat surface, with the fore and after ends placed against the ends of the midside, and check the whole assembly for mirror image. Cut out four buttstraps, ⅜ inch by 4 inches by 16 inches, from the plywood sheet used for the bottom layout, or use scrap pieces. Draw a centerline lengthwise on each buttstrap and align that centerline with the joint. Don't use any glue yet; just get the strap on the joint and carefully mark the center location.

Take a piece of scrap, butt it right up next to the buttstrap, and tack it to the top and bottom of the side, watching closely to make sure the buttstrap

Karin fastens one of the buttstraps, made from scrap plywood.

93

doesn't move. If you want to be tidy, put a piece of waxed paper under the joint. Now spread glue on the buttstrap and on the plywood side where it is going, and place the buttstrap back against the tacked scrap of wood for perfect alignment. This technique works in many places; the scrap piece is called a backing block. Using a backing block is the safe way when you want to be sure that a slippery piece of glued wood doesn't move on you. Grab a handful of 1-inch number 14 smooth wire copper nails and drive them into the buttstrap and right through the side into the floor (if it's your own) or into a piece of scrap wood. Fasten both buttstraps, setting the nailheads slightly, then pull the side clear from whatever it was resting on. Stand the side on edge between your legs, hold a light maul (3 to 5 pounds) against the nail heads, and hammer the protruding nail points over in the direction of the woodgrain. Wipe off the excess glue, and your sides are ready for the waterline.

Look at the waterline layout again and note that it is laid out in 1-foot intervals for 8 feet on the midsides and extends a foot on each of the side ends. Place your rule exactly 1 foot aft from the center of the butt joint and lay off a distance of 10 feet. Take a try-square and put a line about 4 inches long at each 1-foot interval. Look at the aft end of the waterline and note that the first measurement is 0, 1, 4 (1½ inches) for the extreme end and the next one is 0, 2, 0. The third measurement is 0, 2, 4 at a six-inch interval and then it is 0, 2, 7 at the butt joint. The measurements continue at 1-foot intervals along the midside to the butt joint. After the butt joint, there is a measurement of 0, 1, 2 at a six-inch interval, then the last two are at 1-foot intervals.

Start marking the waterline at the stern with the 0, 1, 4 measure, measuring up from the bottom edge and *writing each waterline height* right on the spot. This will help avoid getting the waterline all marked off and then discovering on rechecking that you've started in the wrong spot or missed a measurement entirely. I've done that once or twice.

Now drive a small brad (that's a skinny nail, about an 18-wire and an inch or so long) at each waterline height mark. Saw out a ½-inch by ½-inch batten and spring it around the nails in a fair curve. Mark along the batten's length, and you've drawn the waterline. Repeat for the other side.

STEP 2: CENTER FRAME AND TEMPORARY FRAMES

Draw the center frame full size directly on the plywood, or on building paper, or on your shop floor. Saw the framing square-edged 2½ inches wide from ¾-inch stock. A stick 6 feet long is enough to make both the side frames and the bottom frame, with a little left over to allow for a mis-cut or poor grain. Cut two pieces of the framing stock 17 inches long (that's an inch longer than the sides are wide, and allows for the angle between the sides and bottom).

To find the angle between the sides and bottom, take a bevel square and lay the handle on the full-size drawing. Holding the handle firmly to keep it from moving, swing the blade until it matches the angle. Tighten the bevel square locking nut. You now have the angle for both the bottom of the side frame and the end of the bottom frame.

You don't have a bevel square? Okay, then, use your eye. That's the best thing you've got going for you anyway, so don't be afraid to use it. This is how the eyeball method works. Lay a piece of the side framing on the drawing right where it goes; then take another piece of the side framing and, using it as a straightedge, lay it on the bottom of the drawing, allowing the end to cross the side frame. Mark along the bottom piece across the side piece, and you have it. I often do it that way rather than bother to hunt for my bevel square, and find

Now the center frame is fastened to one of the sides.

95

it even more accurate at times, because using a longer approach to a shortcut is better than vice versa.

With the framing all cut, the centerline marked, and the frame laid out on your full-size drawing, make the gussets and lay them on top of the framing, eying them for fit and marking their locations for gluing. Apply glue to the gussets and the framing pieces, and nail them all together with 1-inch bronze anchor nails. Cut the limber holes, and you've finished the center frame, except for the curved top part of the side frame, which you can do later if you hesitate to cut it off at the time of assembly.

Temporary Frames

The temporary frames are shown with their locations and dimensions on the numbered construction plan. If you have any scrap plywood around, ⅜ inch or heavier, it's easier and faster to make them from this, in one piece, rather than using the sawed and braced frame method. There's not much to these temporary frames; just make them to the dimensions given, and bevel the sides of the forward frame 20 degrees and the after frame 23 degrees. Be sure to mark them "forward" and "aft" for their respective locations.

STEP 3: STERN AND STEM POSTS

Saw the stern and stem posts from 1½-inch stock, saving the scrap edges for later use when clamping. The stem post is sawed 28 degrees—the sternpost, 30½ degrees. Make both posts about 20 inches long to allow plenty of length at the ends when fastening them to the sides.

STEP 4: SIDES AND CENTER FRAME ASSEMBLY

Stand the sides on edge, bottom up, and bore holes about 3 inches or less apart through the sides at the center frame location, from the inside out. Apply glue to the edges of the center frame and bring it against one side, checking to see that the edge of the frame is exactly on the frame line and the bottom of the frame is flush with the edge of the side. Holding it carefully in place or using a backing block, bore back through the uppermost hole into the frame and drive in a 1¼-inch anchor nail. Check the end of the frame toward the floor to see if it has slipped sideways; if not, fasten it near the end. Now drive the rest of the nails home. Repeat the operation on the other side.

Sides and center frame have been assembled.

STEP 5: FASTENING THE STEM AND STERN POSTS

Locate the stern post on one of the sides and dry-fit it (no glue), leaving the ends projecting past the sides about an equal distance. Hold the post in place and clamp or tack a backing block right up against it. While the stern post is in place, draw a line across it, along the sheer and chine, to serve as a guide for the glue. Apply the glue and place the post back against the block, fastening it to the side with 1⅛-inch nails. Now repeat the operation for the stem post.

Take the pieces of scrap you saved from the stem and tack one on the outside edge of the side as shown at the bottom of the plywood layout plan.

Saw the other scrap piece into 3-inch lengths and nail them to the outside of the other side, similarly aligned, spaced to permit starting of permanent nails. These temporary pieces will give you a place to set up your clamps to hold the ends in when the sides are brought together.

STEP 6: GETTING IT ALL TOGETHER

Tack the aft temporary frame to one side *aft* of the buttstrap and the forward temporary frame *forward* of the buttstrap. The ends should be pulled in somewhat when you do this, rather than letting one end fly while fastening the other. Cut eight small blocks three inches long by an inch or so wide, nothing fussy. Nail two to each side of the sheer and chine near the temporary frame. When you pull the sides in with the Spanish windlass, these blocks will keep it from slipping when it is wound up. (What's a Spanish windlass? It's just a piece of rope tied around whatever two pieces are to be pulled together, and would up with a stick, just like a tourniquet.) Bring the sides together so the temporary frame is touching the other side, and tack the other side in place. Apply glue to the stern post and pull the ends in by hand until you can get a couple of clamps on them; pull them in the rest of the way with the clamps. Repeat for the bow.

Pulling the sides in and landing them fairly on the end posts is probably the most exciting and trickiest part of the building process, but the effort is amply rewarded when you step back and see what were once separate, straight-edged flat pieces suddenly turned into a three-dimensional object of beauty, with curves. *It's a boat!* You have finished the hardest part now. From here on, it's just a matter of adding pieces a step at a time until the job is finished.

STEP 7: CHINES AND GUNWALES

The chines and gunwales are next, so let's get to it by going to the local lumberyard and selecting a 14-foot 2 x 4 for stock. Of course, it takes more lumber than that to complete the boat—see the materials list on the plan sheet showing the amounts and sizes needed. But for sake of clarity, we will deal with what we are using right now at this stage of construction.

Don't ask the salesman for a 14-foot 2 x 4 expecting that he will pass you just what you want. Get right on the pile yourself and look for the best, straightest-grain, free-from-knots 2 x 4 you can find. And while you are doing it, show courtesy to the lumberyard people by being neat in your hunting habits. The best 2 x 4s or boards, for some reason or other, are usually on the bottom of the pile (I think they hide them there purposely), so when you take the pile apart, put it back together again just as you found it. Otherwise, you

The temporary frames are in place forward and aft, and the sides have been pulled together with a Spanish windlass.

aren't likely to be welcomed back to pick over the pile again.

You might wonder why lumberyard owners are so sensitive about having their piles of lumber neatly stacked; the reason is more than cosmetic. Lumber stacked outdoors has spacers between the layers of boards so that the green lumber will air-dry properly. The spacers are placed at intervals close enough to support the weight of successive layers without one board touching the other. The spacers, too, are placed directly one over the other, so their load-bearing is distributed evenly down through the pile. Along comes the uncaring or knows-no-better lumber hunter, who decides he wants that board there in the middle of the pile. So he throws the top layers every which way and grabs his board out of the middle and goes off with it, leaving the lumberyard owner to send a man to rebuild the pile again. If left helter-skelter out in the weather, the lumber would soon look like a pile of pretzels, and it would be unsalable to any other customer. So be courteous about it. Put the pile back exactly the way you found it, and chances are you will be allowed to keep your privilege of picking over the pile.

Most 2 x 4s measure 1½ inches by 3½ inches these days, and come in even-numbered lengths from 8 feet to 16 feet, planed four sides with the corners rounded. One piece of 2 x 4 by 14 feet is necessary to make the gunwales and chines. When you saw the gunwales, you might as well take advantage of the rounded corners and take one gunwale off each edge of the 2 x 4. Saw the four pieces for the chines out of the remainder. Saw the gunwales and chines ½ inch thick. Now crank your table saw to 13 degrees, put two chines together, and run them through the saw, putting the bottom bevel on both chines in one pass. If the chines are to be taped, return the tablesaw to perpendicular and take just a sixteenth or less off the side of the outside chine to leave a shoulder for the tape to butt against.

Fair the bottom edges of the hull sides flat athwartships (use your block plane and straightedge) before the chines are put on; otherwise you will have to cut down both the chines and the plywood edge together for a flat bottom fit.

Place the hull upside down on sawhorses at a convenient working height, leaving the temporary frames in place, and apply glue to the side of the chine going next to the hull and the side of the outside chine going next to that. Put both chine pieces together, and, starting at the stern post, clamp the chine to the side, leaving a little of the chine running out by the ends (no need for any end fit here). Place your clamps about a foot apart as you work forward.

With a $\frac{5}{64}$-inch drill bit, drill holes from the inside into the chine, 4 or 5 inches apart, the whole length of the chine, staggering the holes. Fasten with 1⅛-inch bronze nails, and drive one at each of the end posts. Repeat for the other side. Saw the ends of the chines off flush, bow and stern. Check the chines for smoothness and athwartship flatness.

STEP 8: FITTING BOTTOM AND BUTTSTRAPS

There are two ways of fitting the Teal's bottom. If the diagramed bottom shown on the plywood layout plan is used, be sure to leave *at least* a half-inch margin all around when cutting out the bottom. Make *sure* that the bottom will cover to the outside of the chines. Fit the bottom *first*, and cut out the other parts shown on the plan later.

That's one way of doing it. The other way, which I use, is easier, faster, and safer; it is to fit the bottom in the same way as the top crust is fitted to a pie. Place the 8-foot bottom sheet equidistant from both ends with a ⅛- or ¼-inch overlap on one chine (according to how much you trust your sawing). Transfer

After gluing and clamping the two chine pieces, Karin uses bronze nails to fasten them.

the frame centerline to the bottom, remove the sheet, and extend the line full length, both sides. Replace the sheet and check to be certain it centers on the frame. Hold it in position with a brad tacked at each side.

Roughly shape the two bottom end tabs with ample side overhang, and butt the ends against the 8-foot sheet. Extend the centerline through the end tabs on both sides; check the alignment along the whole length. If all three pieces are not aligned, remove one brad and swing the bottom sideways until the end-tab centerlines line up through the end posts. Tack the plywood sheet in place. To locate each buttstrap, mark a centerline lengthwise on a piece of ⅜-inch plywood that is 4 inches wide and long enough to overhang the chines. Lift the

101

Using the portable circular saw to cut out the bottom piece.

end of the bottom sheet to slip the strap into place, draw your pencil along the inside of the sides for the athwartship fit, and cut the strap to allow ⅛-inch slack between the strap ends and the hull sides. Apply glue and replace the strap without removing the bottom sheet. Position the end tabs and glue and fasten them with copper nails.

Now trace around the hull shape on the underside of the bottom overhang. Remove the bottom and set your Skilsaw to 13 degrees. Cut the bottom to shape but leave the line for insurance. The closer you dare come to the line, the less edge planing you will have to do. Replace the bottom, check the centerline, and mark the chines to locate the center frame.

Apply glue liberally to the chines; put the bottom on, tacking it to the end posts. Check the centerline, and use the chine marks to draw a line across the bottom to indicate frame position. Nail the bottom to the chines, starting from the center toward the ends, using 1¼-inch nails. Fasten the gunwales with ⅞-inch nails and remove the temporary frames.

STEP 9: FIBERGLASS-TAPING THE CHINES

If the chines are to be taped, do it now before the bottom shoe is put on. An electric hand plane is fast and easy for removing excess bottom edge. A

The forward buttstrap is fastened to the bottom.

103

low-angle block plane will finish the rest down flush to the sides. Edge grain is tough to cut by hand. If you find the plane is dragging a bit, rub paraffin wax on the bottom; it will do wonders. Paraffin, by the way, is also great for loosening saws that bind and slicking up other tools around the shop.

Round the edges ⅜ inch or a little more, and she's ready for taping. Starting at one end, lay a roll of 3-inch fiberglass tape, allowing some overhang. Stick an awl through the end to hold it to the bottom, and run the tape to the bow, stretching it tight; hold it there with another awl. Mix some resin, saturate the cloth, and work the edge tightly into the lip you cut for it in Step 7. If puckers appear in the tape, remove one of the awls and stretch the tape a little, then

Fiberglass taping the chines. The awl in the foreground holds the tape securely to the bottom.

Karin applies resin over the fiberglass tape on the stem. The chines have already been coated with resin. Tacks are placed 4 or 5 inches apart to help secure the cloth.

stick the awl in again and put on another coat of resin right away. Let the resin set up a little, and then drive staples or tacks 4 or 5 inches apart to help hold the cloth. There is never any problem with bonding glass to plywood, but for some reason it doesn't stick well to spruce (maybe the pitch in the spruce is the problem), so it's good practice to fasten the tape in place.

STEP 10: SHOE AND SKEG

Make the shoe 1½ inches square by 11 or 12 feet long. Set your tablesaw rip guide at ¾ inch and split the shoe for 1, 7, 4 (that's a lengthwise cut, 1 foot 7½ inches long, for the skeg to fit into). Stop the cut a little short of the mark, or

105

the cut will be longer on the underside. Finish the cut with a handsaw.

Cut the skeg 2 feet 2 inches long from a piece of 2 x 4. To make the scarph in the skeg to match the cutout in the shoe, lay the notched section of the shoe right on the skeg just as it looks on the hull profile plan. Trace around the shoe, and saw out the skeg. Glue and fasten the skeg with a few 1¼-inch nails. Round the end of the skeg to your fancy. To fasten the shoe, bore through the bottom along the centerline, alternating each side of the centerline with holes spaced 4 or 5 inches apart. Draw a parallel line half the width of the shoe from the centerline as a placement guide. It's handy to have a helper hold the shoe against this line, moving a weight along it for a backing as each nail is driven from inside. The skeg is also fastened from the inside, with three 2-inch number 14 bronze flathead screws backed up by a few smaller ones. Prebore the holes with a Screwmate of appropriate size. Cut off the bow end of the shoe, rounding it nicely. Make a block about 1½ by 2½ inches, square, shaped to fit over the stern post, to take the upper rudder gudgeon.

That completes the outside of the hull. Now we can turn her right-side up and get on with the interior.

If you want a rowing version, skip the rest of this chapter, add the rowing seat, the bow and stern thwarts, and call her done. I suspect the skeg should be kept, though, to keep her rowing straight.

STEP 11: MAST STEP AND PARTNER

We'll sail this one, so let's keep on going, making and locating the mast step next. That's number 12 on the keyed notes of the construction profile plan; it calls for a piece of 7-inch-square ⅜-inch plywood mounted on two 1½- by 1½-inch supports. Find the center of the square and make a 1¾-inch-square hole for the mast. Center the step athwartships. Its fore-and-aft location is 3 feet 7½ inches from the forward side of the center frame to the after side of the stepped mast. Mark around the step supports, and bore down through the bottom for the fastenings. Apply glue to the step and place it back on the marks. Fasten from the outside with 1¼-inch nails.

The mast partner is ¾ inch by 5½ inches by 3 feet. Find its center and make the mast hole. Level your boat athwartships, place the partner on the gunwales, and measure 3 feet 6 inches from the forward side of the center frame to the after side of the mast at the top of the partner. Check to see if the ends are going askew by measuring the distance between the partner edge and the buttstrap edge at each end.

When you're satisfied with the partner's location, mark the spot on the gunwales, remove the partner, and cut the tops of the gunwales flat across so the partner has good bearing. Put the partner back, place your level on the step and partner centerlines, and adjust until the level shows plumb. Put position marks on the gunwales and partner, apply glue, put back the partner, and fasten it with long, thin wood screws.

Cut and fasten the after thwart, make the rowing seat with ½ inch concavity, fasten the foot braces (key number 15), and that completes the interior. So much for major steps; now for the appurtenances you need for sail.

THE RUDDER

Make the rudder from ½-inch plywood 1 foot wide and 3 feet 6 inches long, laid off in 3-inch squares as shown on the sail plan. Note that the leading edges

Establishing the athwartship alignment of the mast partner and the relationship of the mast partner to the step.

and the lower trailing edges are parallel and represent the full width of the plywood. To find the angle along the trailing edge that reaches almost to the top of the rudder, use the 1½-inch scale on your scale rule and measure from the extreme lower edge of the rudder to where the angle begins; put a mark there. Notice that the line to be drawn ends a little forward of the tiller bolt hole, down exactly one square and in one square plus two-thirds of another (or 4¾ inches measured in horizontally from the leading edge).

Draw a straight line between those points, and draw the curve on the after part of the rudder head by eye, noting that the extreme width of the top is two squares, or six inches. For the rounded lower leading edge, measure in from the edge of the plywood from the bottom or the side, or both; drive in some brads and spring a very light batten around them to draw the curve.

Fair in about 3 inches as shown along the leading and trailing edges, carrying the taper no higher than the wetted surface to keep strength in the upper part of the rudder. The leading edge can be made blunter than the trailing edge to offer some protection from striking objects, but the trailing edge should be fairly sharp to keep the pintles from chattering in the gudgeons.

The rudder is tapered easily with an electric hand plane and finished smooth with a belt sander using a 60-grit belt. The tiller is made from spruce or fir, ¾ inch by 2½ inches by 3 feet 6 inches; it is held in position with a ¼-inch by 3-inch machine bolt.

THE LEEBOARD

Make the leeboard from ½-inch plywood, 1 foot wide and 4 feet long. Draw a centerline the length of the piece of plywood and adjust a compass to a radius of half the width of the leeboard. Set the compass pivot on the centerline at a point that allows the pencil point to reach the end of the leeboard. Swing the compass to form an arc, which will define the bottom of the board. Cut it out according to the plan.

Make two tongues ¾ inch by 1½ inches by 2 feet to the shape shown in the plan. Stand the leeboard against the boat's side with its centerline lined up with the center frame. Place the two tongues against the side of the hull, one on each side of the center frame, and measure for the thickness of the leeboard blocking. The blocking has to be slightly thicker than the gunwale thickness because of gunwale curvature. Measure the blocking location with your rule, fasten the tongues to the lower blocking with ¼-inch by 4-inch bolts, and the upper part of the tongues with one long screw each.

Put the leeboard back in place. It won't go down? It's loose enough at the top, but as it goes down, it binds? That's because the gunwale is ½ inch and the chine is 1 inch, which causes a wedge effect. Let the board lie where it will, set your compass at ⅛ inch or so, and scribe the tongues. Take off wood a little at a time until the board goes all the way down. Now you have a nice fit—the board is still loose enough at the top for easy placement, yet it tightens as it goes down, so it won't rattle when it's in place. If it seems too tight, take a little more off the tongues or rub some paraffin wax on them.

Fair the edges of the leeboard all around as shown. To hold the board down in use, put a small screw eye on the lower leeboard blocking. This will take a short length of twine tied down to a 2-inch cleat mounted conveniently on the center side frame.

GUDGEONS AND PINTLES

Strap gudgeons will be the handiest if you can get them, but it seems "they don't make them anymore," so here's how to make your own gudgeons that will fit ½-inch pintles (still obtainable; Wilcox-Crittenden makes them).

Buy a couple of ¼-inch by 4-inch brass or bronze eye bolts with a shoulder. Cut about a ⅜-inch length of ¼-inch brass pipe, drive it through the eye, and upset the ends with a ball-peen hammer. The pipe will take up the slack in the eye to make a good pintle fit. For a top gudgeon, bore through the stern post with an undersize drill, dip the bolt in glue, drive it through the post, and fasten it with a nut and washer. For the lower gudgeon, taper the bolt to a fairly sharp point on a grinding wheel, bore into the skeg for about half the bolt's length, dip the bolt in glue, and drive it home.

HANGING THE RUDDER

To hang the rudder, place it against the gudgeons at the height shown on the sail plan and mark the tops of the gudgeon locations on the rudder. Cut ⅜ to ½ inch off the end of the top pintle and place the bottom of the pintle strap on the top mark. Place the other pintle on the lower mark. Hang the rudder and adjust the pintles for easy removal. Mark the pintle strap location. Take the rudder off, cut a 3-inch number 9 copper nail (leaving the head on) long enough to reach through the strap, and leave ⅛ inch for upsetting. Bore through the strap and the rudder, push the nail through, slip a number 9 copper burr (a thin copper washer) over the end and upset it. Repeat for the bottom pintle. Slip the tiller over the rudder head, bore through both, slip the bolt through, and your rudder is hung.

THE MAST

Make the mast from pine, spruce, or most anything at hand that's reasonably free from poor grain and knots. The sail plan shows a mast 1¾ inches square in section tapered to ¾ inch, by 15 feet 8½ inches overall. Most 2 x 4s come

Karin rivets the pintles to the rudder.

planed now to 1½ inches—a bit too light for the mast. If you are near a sawmill, you probably can pick a piece 2 inches in the rough and have it planed 1¾ inches, or you can laminate what you need from two pieces.

Lay out the stick on a couple of horses, put a centerline on it, and lay off the taper as shown on the sail plan. Cut the taper on a bandsaw or tablesaw, lay the mast down again, and turn it so the side the wood has been taken from is facing up. Lay off the taper again, cut it, and smooth up the saw mark. Do this until all four sides are tapered, then round the corners ¼ inch.

Number 5 on the sail plan shows two cleats, one on each side of the mast to hold the eyesplice or loop. Make these cleats about six inches long and an inch wide, with tapered ends. Mark the centers of the cleats and notch them with a rattail file deep enough to take the ⅜-inch Dacron rope sling; put an eyesplice in one end of the sling large enough to slide over the mast. Splice a one-inch sailmaker's thimble in the other end, keeping the overall length of the sling as short as possible (about 8 or 9 inches). If you can't splice, tie a bowline in each end.

Slip the eye over the mast, locating it 3 feet 6 inches from the end. Glue the cleats, tuck the rope in the notches, and fasten the cleats. It's easier doing it that way than it is trying to make the splice around the mast.

THE SPRIT

Make the sprit 9 feet 6 inches overall, 1⅝ inches square, tapered to ⅞ inch each end. Cut a ¼-inch by 2-inch slot at each end to take the knotted ends of the clew pennant sheet and snotter, and round the edges ¼ inch.

RIGGING YOUR BOAT

To rig the sail, bore a hole athwartships one inch from the head of the mast and tie your first grommet at the head of the sail. Tie each grommet with number 300 braided nylon, or something else fairly stout, backing the tie with a couple of overhand knots down close. Cut and sear the ends with a rope-cutting gun.

Cut a piece of ¼-inch Dacron line about 4 feet long for the snotter, and tie a stopper knot in the end. Fasten a 3-inch cleat to the mast about 9 inches above the mast partner. Your sheet is a 14-foot length of ¼-inch Dacron with a stopper knot to catch under the clew pennant in the boom slot. To set the sail, catch the boom on the knot tied in the sheet under the clew pennant. Catch the snotter knot in the slot at the other end of the boom, lead the snotter through the thimble, pull down on the snotter to tighten the foot of the sail, and fasten the snotter to the cleat on the mast. To keep the luff taut, tie a piece of nylon in the grommet at the foot of the sail and lead it down to a 2-inch cleat just above the partner.

Furl the sail by rolling the leech taut, while you twist up at the clew. This will make a tight furl, which can be secured with a single gasket near the foot.

FLOTATION

Even swamped, Teal floats high on her side without any flotation, but the addition of flotation will make bailing easy and will help to right her. If you

Time to rig the Teal for the first sail. (P.S. It was a solid success.)

want flotation, simply cut urethane blocks roughly tapered to fit in each end. Wedge or lash them in place so they are readily removable, and glue wood slats on top of them for appearance. Keep your flotation raised off the bottom 3 or 4 inches to provide room for stowage, the ends of oars, etc. A fiberglass cloth and epoxy coating will keep gulls from eating any exposed foam.

Now go back to Chapter 7, and get out your paint brushes. Hope you enjoyed building her. Sailing her is even more fun.

10

Rounding Out the Instant Fleet

Though all the Instant Boats are built basically the same way, there are minor differences among them, mostly in the relative ease of laying out some of the hull shapes full size on the plywood sheets, and the ease of bending on gunwale and chine strips.

In this chapter we will deal with the basic layouts of each boat, and flag trouble spots to watch for as the construction progresses. Some short cuts are safe, and some aren't.

THE ELEGANT PUNT

You need only two sheets of ¼-inch by 8-foot plywood for the Punt. Both sides as well as the bow and stern transoms are cut from one sheet. The bottom, fore and aft seat, and midship frame all come from the second sheet.

To get the shape for the sides, line off the sheet crosswise at 6-inch intervals, then measure along each line from the edge of the sheet to locate points for the bottom and sheer curves. Drive nails at the sheer and chine points and spring a batten around the nails to draw the curves. Don't bother laying off the waterline as shown; just measure one inch up on the ends and draw a line straight across. It will improve the appearance of the boat and give the waterline a happy look.

Nail the midship frame to the sides. Then nail the sides to the transoms, and put on the gunwales and chines. Make these ¾ inch by 1⅛ inches in cross-

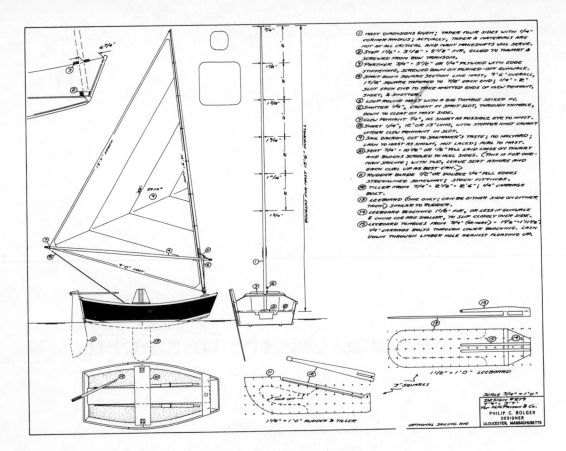

Above, below, and opposite: *Numbered instruction plans for the Elegant Punt.*

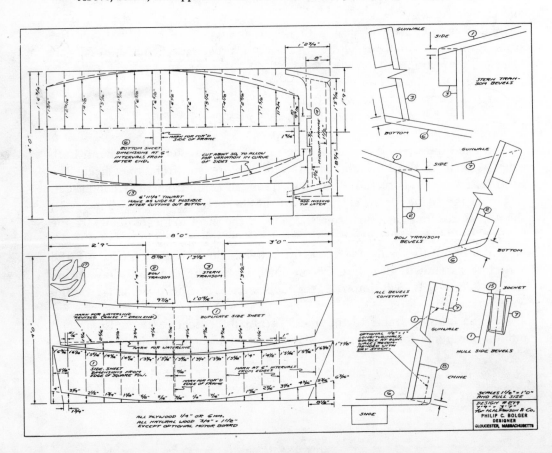

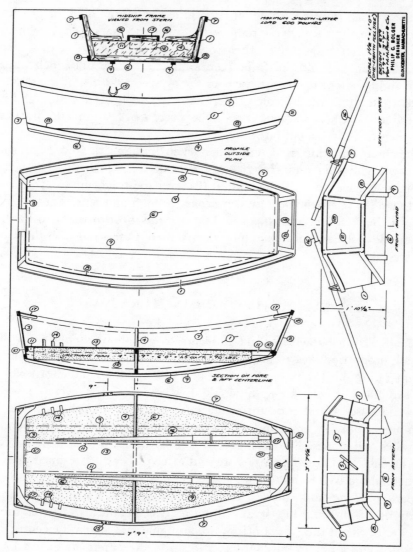

section rather than the ¾ inch by 1½ inches shown on the drawing. Bending on these strips is the hardest part of building the Punt, and ¾ inch by 1⅛ inches is about maximum for making the two-way bend in such a short length.

Put the bottom on next—there is no need to lay out for rough bottom fit first as shown on the plan. Make sure your centerlines are drawn on the transoms and the midship frame. Support the transoms on sawhorses with the ends level to avoid building a twist in her when you put the bottom on. Lay the ¼-inch by 8-foot sheet for the bottom right where it goes, leaving ⅛-inch or

115

¼-inch overlap by the chine at the midship frame, and mark the frame centerline on the sheet. Now remove the sheet and mark its centerline on both sides at its full length. (Another way to do this, which saves a step, is to measure from the midship frame centerline to ⅛ inch or ¼ inch outside the chine and transfer the measurement to the plywood sheet. Put the sheet on and check to see that the bottom centerline meets with the transom and midship centerlines.) With the plywood sheet in place, mark around the bottom, then take the sheet off and cut out the bottom.

The important things to remember when building this boat are: (1) don't make the gunwales and chines any heavier than ¾ inch by 1⅛ inch (that's before you have beveled the chine); (2) level the transoms to avoid a built-in twist; and (3) relate the bottom centerline to the frame centerlines.

Both the Elegant Punt and the Teal are the most difficult to build of the Instant Boat fleet as far as bending is concerned. Compared with these two, the rest are easy.

SURF—15-FOOT 6-INCH CRAB SKIFF

The Surf is *my* favorite, and it seems to me about as perfect a blend of overall proportions as I could ever expect to see in so simple a shape. Her weight of around 150 pounds isn't all that much, either, and allows car-topping for a couple of average-strength people. I've used mine for several seasons, and I am well pleased with her performance and her ability to carry a couple of adults with plenty of room and comfort. She's easy to build with no hard bends in the gunwales and chines. Four sheets of ¼-inch by 8-foot plywood are all you need for the sides and bottom, with fore and after pieces buttstrapped just forward of the midship web frame.

Mark out the hull sides to the given dimensions, and on them mark the locations of the midship frame and the two bulkheads. Fasten the 6-inch buttstraps. Stand the sides bottom-up, and glue and fasten the center frame to the sides, checking carefully for exact location. Next, put the forward and after bulkheads temporarily in place. Bring the sides in to the transom and stem, and fasten them. Remove the two bulkheads, apply glue, and put them back, making sure they stand flush with the bottom edges of the sides. The chines and bottom are next; follow the procedure described for the Teal and the Elegant Punt.

When you get to the bowsprit-mast partner, paint the forward compartment first and install a bow eye just below the cutwater. Then fit your deck and nail it to the partner. Fill the compartment with a dense type of Styrofoam or urethane, and *then* nail down the deck, closing it forever. (Remember, the slot in the end of the bowsprit is just to hold an anchor line for temporary

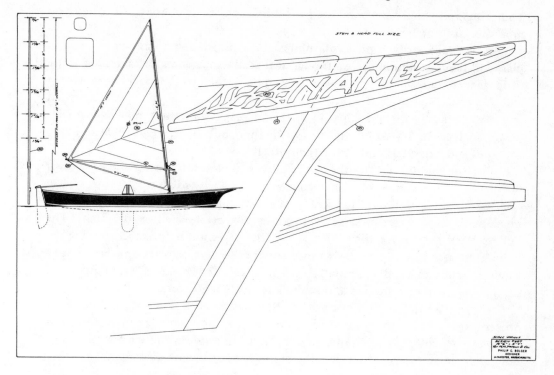

Above and below: *Numbered instruction plans for the Surf.*

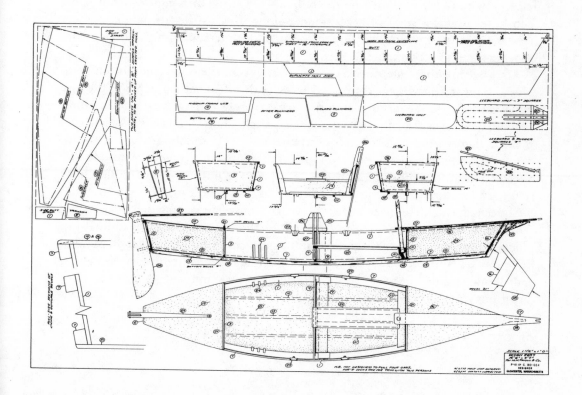

anchoring and should never be used for leaving the boat unattended. When you moor her, use the bow eye.)

For the trailboards, a piece of ¼-inch plywood shaped as shown on the sail plan will bend around nicely, although it is really something to carve. Make it a little deeper than shown, for it will have to be scribed to fit under the gunwales and bowsprit. You can't copy the trailboard exactly and expect it to fit anyway, because you are copying on a flat plane something that has to fit a curve, so leave extra wood on the top of the trailboards, bend them in along the sides and cutwater, and scribe them to fit.

Doing the fancy work on the Surf's bow is the hardest part of the project. It doesn't have to be done, but what you gain in looks is worth it.

A word on waterlines: Builders of the Teal and Punt don't have to bother much with their waterlines, as they are already established on the plans. The builder need only mark them directly on the plywood before constructing the hull. The Surf plans—as well as those for the Zephyr, Kayak, and Schooner— show no ready-marked waterline, so we must establish it ourselves, taking it off the sail plan with a scale rule and striking it on the completed hull.

I will explain the method for putting the waterline on the Surf, and the same procedure works for the others: First we have to find the ends of the waterline. Look at the sail plan and note that the waterline doesn't extend clear to the bow and the stern, but intersects the chine at points some distance from them. The points in the middle do not matter, as long as we can see where they end.

To find out the locations of the waterline ends, pick up your scale rule and take a look at the sail plan for the scale. It says "scale various," which doesn't tell us much, so lay your rule on the hull and try the ¾-inch-equals-1-foot scale. You know that the Surf is 15 feet 6 inches long. If the scale fits, you know you have the right one. It's no big mystery, but you sometimes wonder why designers aren't more explicit.

Anyway, use the scale rule to measure back from the bow along the chine to where the waterline intersects it, and transfer this distance full scale to the hull chine itself. Repeat, working from the stern; then level your boat athwartships.

Now, at each end of the waterline tack a stick, about 3 feet by 1½ inches by ¾ inch, right to the hull so that it extends out horizontally at right angles to the hull centerline, with the top of its inboard end exactly marking the intersection of the chine and waterline. Support the outboard ends so that both sticks are absolutely level and firmly braced against the floor.

Stretch a chalkline over the tops of the two sticks, parallel to the hull centerline. Next, pull the line in from either the bow or the stern until it just touches the boat's side amidships, and push in a thumbtack under the line at this point of contact. Now you can work the line from the center toward either end. Working alone, it takes too much running back and forth to work in both directions from the center.

Pull the line in against the hull just a few inches ahead or astern of the first point of contact, making sure that it doesn't roll down the sides, and put in another thumbtack. Pull in again, place another thumbtack. Repeat the process until you reach the end of the waterline. Now go back to the center and work toward the other end.

Once the waterline is established, step back and check it for fairness. Your chalkline should lie snugly against the hull with no quick dips or bumps in it.

When satisfied that the waterline looks right, take a pencil and mark small dashes about 3 inches apart under the string the length of the waterline. Take the string off the hull and pull out the thumbtacks. Use a ruler or stick about a foot long and connect all the dashes to produce one solid line. The job is finished. Put on masking tape, and she's ready to paint.

It's easier and faster to have someone helping you to put on the waterline, because one person can keep pulling the string in while the other is placing the tacks, but the above method is the best way of doing it alone. Another way is to use a level, but I think it is a slower and more cumbersome method.

All of the Instant Boats have sides that stand quite plumb, which makes it easy to put on a waterline. The hard ones are boats with more side flare, or with vee bottoms.

Ordinarily, waterlines begin and end at the extreme ends of a boat, and in that case a stick that is long enough can be nailed to the bow and transom so the waterline can be struck without shifting the set-up, but some of the Instant Boats, like the Surf, are different, so we change our approach to suit. All waterlines aren't always put on straight, either. Some, like the Teal's, have a bit of rocker to them to give more eye appeal. It all depends on the designer's or builder's taste.

A rockered waterline is no harder to do than a dead straight one. When the Teal plans first arrived from Phil Bolger, the only waterline shown was the one on the sail plan. By picking up the sail plan and sighting the waterline edgewise, I could see it showed plenty of rocker. To find out how much was just a matter of laying a straightedge on the waterline ends and measuring the distance to the deepest part of the rocker, which is just aft of the leeboard. Measuring with the scale rule at ¾-inch scale shows a 2-inch dip in the waterline. All that was required to reproduce the waterline as shown was to pull the chalkline in against the hull at the greatest depth of rocker, then pull the chalkline down 2 inches at that point, drive in a tack over the top of the chalkline, and begin working the waterline in both directions from the original point of contact. That was how I did it. Later I took the waterline off by bending a stiff batten around the hull and spiling the waterline on it. Then I drew the waterline to scale on a piece of paper and sent it off to Phil, who in turn diagramed it on the Teal's plan, thus saving future boatbuilders from all the business of messing with it.

119

ZEPHYR

The larger they get, the easier they are to build, and the 20-foot 9-inch Zephyr is no exception to this rule. When the builder springs the gunwales and chines on this one, he finds there is nothing to it. Four sheets of ⅜-inch by 8-foot plywood are needed for the sides and bottom, along with some 2 x 4s for framing.

The sides are cut out easily the same way as the Teal's by cutting two of the sheets into 16-inch-wide panels—there is no need for any edge measurements to get the sheer and bottom rocker, as was the case with the Surf. Just straight cuts are all you need to get out your sides. The forward and after side pieces are joined to the two completed panels by buttstraps and are placed bottom-up, ready for the midframe and bulkheads, following the same building procedure as with the other Instant Boats.

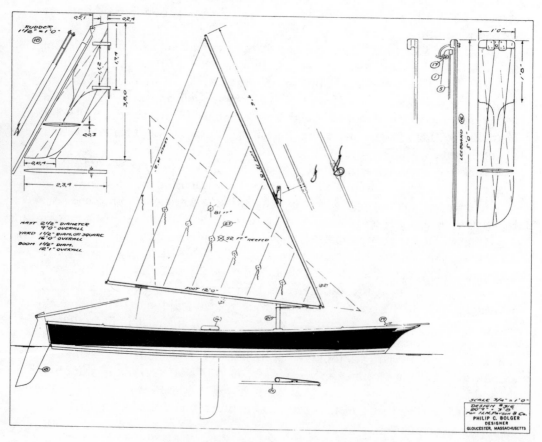

Above and opposite: *Plans for the Zephyr.*

If you can't find 2 x 4s long enough to make the gunwales and chines in one piece, use shorter ones and make a tapered splice in them. Glue these scarph joints well, letting the glue set up hard before you install them.

The leeboard and rudder call for a glued lamination of natural wood (fir, mahogany, etc.), ½ inch by 5½ inches, to finish one inch thick. It probably makes sense in terms of strength to make them as shown on the plans, but it seemed like a lot of work to me, so I made them from two pieces of ½-inch plywood glued together and used all the clamps I could find for good clamping pressure. I've sailed the Zephyr for several seasons now without breaking either the rudder or the leeboard, but maybe I'm just lucky. Anyway, I prefer taking a chance on breakage rather than doing that much extra work. In use, they appear to have ample strength.

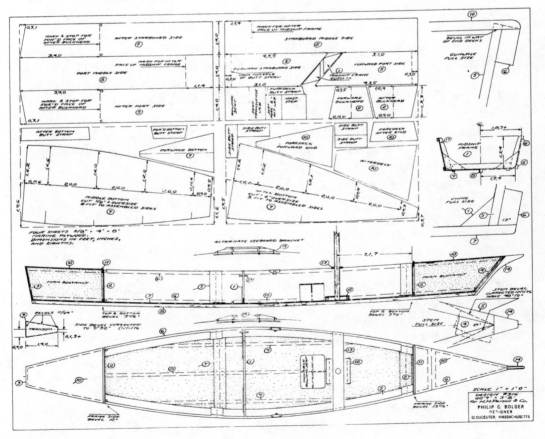

THE 12-FOOT KAYAK

Phil Bolger laid the Kayak out in his head one day while paddling Kotick (a small, planked-up canoe I made for him a few years back). It's the only boat in the Instant fleet that calls for 12-foot plywood. Quarter-inch by 12-foot sheets aren't easy to come by at the local lumberyard, but they should be available at any marine lumber supplier. If not, two ¼-inch by 8-foot sheets will do, with a little waste of material, and a small difference in price.

If 8-foot plywood is used, lay out the sides and bottom so the buttstraps are aft of the after coaming and they will be out of sight. The buttstraps could be forward, but there they might interfere with sliding your legs in and out.

Lay out the diagramed side on the 12-foot plywood, measuring from the edge of the sheet. Mark the bottom centerline next, making sure it is properly located as shown on the plans. We can save some time here by not laying off the bottom shape, but I recommend that only for those who trust themselves not to wander too far when cutting out the sides. There isn't much room there, and sloppy cutting of the sides could rob the bottom. Carefully cut out one side and clean up the edges with a plane, and then use it as a pattern to cut out the other side. Next cut out the forward and after bulkheads. Then place the sides upside-down and fasten the bulkheads.

Pull the ends in and fasten them at the stem and the stern. Put the chines and gunwales on, and you're ready for the bottom. Place the plywood sheet on the boat with bottom centerline lined up through the bow and stern centers. Tack the sheet to the chines to hold it in place, and mark around the chines for bottom fit. Take the bottom off, saw it out, and put it back. Easy, right? And all that laying off of the bottom was saved. You have to be careful, though, doing it the easy way. If you have any doubts, play it safe and lay out the diagramed bottom as shown.

The large cockpit allows ample room for a six-footer without shoehorning him in, and it guarantees easy exit in case of a capsize. Speaking of that, however, getting into her is a bit tricky, and is best done from a float. Get in a crouch position and slide your legs in while holding on to the float. Trying to step into one of these things from an upright position invites disaster, as I was privileged to observe one day when a young lobster fisherman asked to try out mine. Stepping in her as casually as he would his wide-bottomed punt, he made one continuous motion in, out, and under. Surfacing through a stream of bubbles, he climbed back on the float, eying the Kayak with new respect. He *carefully* lowered himself into place and struck off.

The trick to staying in one of these things, once afloat, is to stay loose. Avoid resting your back against the coaming, and keep your upper body upright, letting the Kayak roll under you.

You can make a cheap paddle from ¼-inch plywood to the dimensions given in Phil Bolger's book *Small Boats,* page 67 (International Marine Publishing

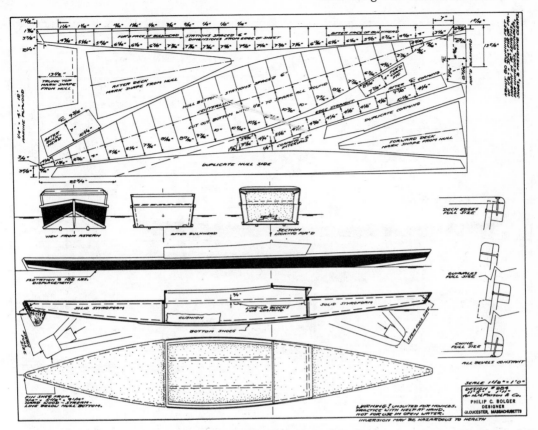

Plans for the 12-foot Kayak.

Company, Camden, Maine). Keep the blade dimensions and paddle length the same, but don't bother trying to make it fancy. Strengthen the paddle with a piece of ¾-inch spruce or whatever, running the spruce out on the blade for more support.

THE FOLDING SCHOONER

It takes 14 sheets of ¼-inch by 8-foot plywood to turn out the Schooner if she is going to be built with ¼ inch throughout, or 10 sheets of ¼-inch plywood and 4 sheets of ⅜ inch if you want the bottom stronger. A bunch of 2 x 4s will do for framing, and four 16-foot-long 2 x 4s glued together will make the masts.

The Schooner isn't hard to build, as she's really only two skiffs put together stern to stern, held together by large deck hinges and a retaining pin. Basically,

123

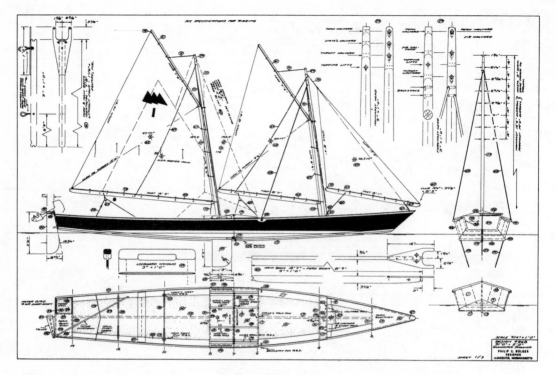

Above, below, and opposite: *Numbered instruction plans for the Folding Schooner.*

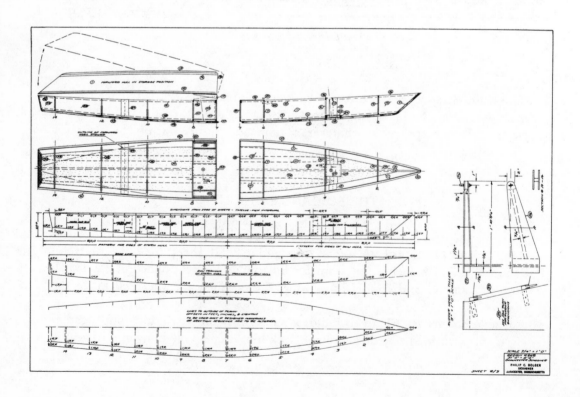

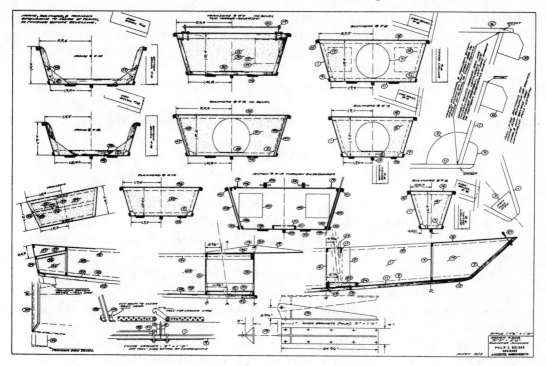

she is built the same as the others, with the exception that she requires more attention to hull alignment. She will take a lot more time to build, though, adding up to roughly 200 hours from start to finish, including the painting.

To ensure she's properly aligned, so the center of the bow lands on the center of the stern when she is folded, the bottoms are put on using the plywood sheets as giant T-squares, fastening the ends and pulling the sides in or out to center the frames.

Bilgeboard Cases. Install the bilgeboard cases before the bottom goes on, marking the location of the slot on the sides and transom so the exact positions can be fixed before you saw them. This you do later after the bottom is nailed on. Have the angle of side and bottom clearly in mind before you saw the slot in the bottom.

Let me tell you about the background of this boat. Having put a lot of time in building the Schooner, I was looking forward to sailing her and giving all those strings a pull. As it turned out, it was more pulling strings than sailing.

The prototype was built for Phil Bolger and was ready for delivery in March of 1973. She was waiting outdoors fully extended, never having been folded. I had all the running rigging ready when Phil arrived so we could bend on the sails and get her ready for launching at the Camden (Maine) Harbor launching ramp the next day. It was quite cold, with a few patches of snow around, so we warmed our hands at frequent intervals over the old woodstove in my shop, dashing back and forth till we got her fully rigged, including the handkerchief-size main staysail.

Satisfied everything looked and worked as it should, we struck the rig, folded her, and put her on the trailer, stowing all the gear in the after section—masts, booms, and gaffs, with halyards still attached—and went in the house for a sip of brandy.

Next day when we struck out for Camden, I had butterflies in my stomach thinking about launching a 31-foot folding schooner for the first time in front of the entire news staff of the *National Fisherman* and any others drawn to watch. A rehearsal would have been nice. But even without it, the Schooner came off the trailer and was launched without incident, except that Phil's overshoes filled with icy cold water the first thing from a larger than usual surge.

A few minutes more and the masts were stepped. Next (in theory) came the raising of the foresail and mainsail, usually accomplished easily enough by a tug on the throat and peak halyards. But you have to be able to find them first, and in this case they were well out of sight and thoroughly scrambled with the rest of the rigging. We got the jib up and I sailed her under jib alone while Phil untangled the mess, finally getting fore and main up just in time to see our audience dwindle down to four—my wife and my mother-in-law, Peter Spectre (editor of International Marine Publishing Company), and a *National Fisher-man* secretary.

Of course we learned a lesson from it, and number 71 of the revised notes on the Schooner plans says all halyards are to engage loops on the gaffs with snap hooks. It's necessary to be able to attach and detach sails, booms, and gaffs easily and quickly, as otherwise a horrible tangle results, which considerably delays getting her rigged again.

The couple of hours that the whole exhibition took was the only time I had for sailing the Schooner, as Phil took her back to Massachusetts with him. It was fun, though, and I found the Schooner fast and responsive.

So there's your whole fleet to choose from—at least until Phil comes up with another idea we both agree is worth developing.

11

Now That You Have Your Instant Boat

Use her! That's the only way to develop the skills you need for seamanlike small-boat handling. If you have never sailed before and feel timid about trying it alone, get a friend to go along with you to teach you how—though I see no reason why you shouldn't try it on your own, since these boats are simple to sail.

There is only one rule you must remember before striking out alone, and that is, *never tie the sheet down*; always leave it free to run out. Strict observation of that one rule can mean the difference between capsizing and staying rightside-up. Sailing one of these light craft comes as naturally as learning to ride a bicycle, and once learned, it is never forgotten.

THE BASICS OF SOLOING

For your first sail, pick a day with the wind light but steady. Assuming you're leaving from a float, set the leeboard and rudder in place, raise the sail, and shove the bow off to catch the wind. As she falls off to leeward, grab the tiller and sheet, put the tiller hard over to leeward, and pull in on the sheet.

At this point the boat will start to gather headway and begin to speed up. Put the tiller amidships to keep her headed just off the wind, and away you go. Bringing the tiller amidships from the leeward position must be done quickly to keep the boat's bow from swinging into the wind, which will cause her to slow down and stall "in irons," or, as she starts to back up, catch the wind on the

The author enjoying a quiet sail aboard one of his Instant Boats. (Photo by Peter H. Spectre)

other side of the sail and put you back into the float again. This can be embarrassing, especially if you are in full view of the group of onlookers who always seem to be on hand to observe the hapless novice. Don't be discouraged, though; just shove off and try it again.

Most of the embarrassing moments in a sailor's life seem to happen when leaving or approaching a dock, float, or mooring. They happen to most of us, me included. For example, when I first stepped straight from my heavy powerboat experience into one of these light things and attempted to dock the Zephyr the very first time, I was looking for her momentum to carry me right to the float and found myself a good oar's length away instead, "in irons," dead in the water and beginning to go backward. I learned right off that there is a world of difference between powerboat handling and sailboat handling when it comes to docking.

You can get a powerboat into a float and look quite good while doing it, by the correct use of the throttle and rudder. If you miss your landing by a small amount, another nudge ahead and one more in reverse will usually get you in without anyone being the wiser. Not so in one of these light sailboats, where the sail is your only power and the sheet is your throttle. They have little momentum, so don't count on that to help dock you or you will find yourself having to go around for another try.

Confidence comes with experience, and, as you gain it, you will find yourself coming in to the float bow on at a good clip, not turning until the bow almost touches, then with split-second timing, quickly putting your tiller hard over and keeping just the right tension on the sheet for the amount of sail power needed to get you alongside the float. Let go of the sheet and you're in there and looking good.

Sailing is such a pleasureful thing that it is difficult to stop thinking about it, but there are other things that should be mentioned. We'll get back to a little more sailing later, but for now, let's heave-to a minute and think about how to park this thing when we're done sailing for the day.

It seems only fitting to complement the simplicity of the Instant Boats by using a small mushroom anchor—say, 25 pounds—for a mooring. On mud bottom, it's heavy enough to hold any of the boats, except for the Schooner, but one of the best features of the mushroom anchor is that it is light enough to be picked up and taken home after a season's use.

After many years of fooling around with heavy outboard and inboard motors, and boats that have to be trailered or hauled, I find I have little use for boats and gear I can't pick up and lug home. I refuse to own a boat trailer now, and I find that I get a lot of pleasure at being able at season's end to throw anchor and all into the 20-foot 9-inch Zephyr, loading boat and all into my pickup, and lugging everything home for winter storage.

There are many ways of rigging a light mooring, but here's how I rig my mushroom so I don't even have to tie or untie a knot when ready to sail. For a 4-foot depth of water at low tide, and about 16 feet at high tide, I use a piece of ¾-inch polypropylene about 30 feet long with an eyesplice around a thimble at each end. Attach one end to the eye of a rod that passes through a plastic mooring buoy about 1 foot in diameter. A piece of 20-foot by ½-inch polypropylene is used for the rider or pendant and has an eyesplice around a thimble at each end. Before both eyesplices are made, slip the rope through a hole in a plastic float large enough to carry the weight of a snap hook, and secure it about three feet or so from the snap-hook end. Use stopper knots on each side of the float, tied in the rider itself. Attach one end of the rider to the eye in the mooring buoy and the other to a snap hook, and you're all set.

Snap hooks bear watching, so don't forget to inspect them frequently for signs of sticking or spring failure. No matter how your mooring is rigged, the most important thing to watch out for is chafe. Where there is a possibility of chafing, make sure it's metal to metal, never rope to metal.

A 25-pound mushroom anchor suitable for most of the boats in the Instant Fleet.

STORAGE AND MAINTENANCE

Not much is required for either storage or maintenance of your Instant Boat. If she has been used in salt water, it's a good idea to wash the hull and all equipment, including the sail, in fresh water. The bottom should be scrubbed as soon as the boat is hauled, before the accumulation of marine growth has a chance to dry. You might not feel like doing it when you're pooped from just hauling her home, but only a few hours in a hot sun or wind will set this growth so hard you will wish you had cleaned it off. Worse still is to leave it until the next season, when you will find it rock hard. So don't put off scrubbing that bottom.

As for storing your boat outside, all you have to do is put her on blocks upside down, and she will keep nicely for the next season.

When the time comes to ready your boat for spring, go over the lashings of your sail for signs of chafe, and check the gudgeons and pintles for wear and cracks.

If you followed the painting procedure in Chapter 7 when you first built your boat, chances are good she won't need much painting; actually, she won't require painting all over for a few years. Bare spots can be touched up (yes, they *will* show), or you can paint her all over with a light coat after first treating the bare spots with an undercoat, sanding, and all that, according to the degree of perfection you want.

I don't see any point, though, in putting on heavy coats of paint year after year whether the boat needs it or not, as some do. It only builds up added weight, not more protection. I'm inclined to go the other way, letting the paint wear off until she really needs painting.

WHERE TO USE YOUR BOAT

I don't recommend the use of any of the Instant Boats in open water. They are not sea boats, nor were they meant to be. The place to use your boat is in sheltered bays, rivers, and the like, where the power of the ocean can't reach you. Those are the best places to learn to sail and to get acquainted with your boat. Protected waters are the places to make your mistakes, not out on open water.

SAFETY TIPS

Regardless of the number of precautions we take to save our necks, probably part of the attraction of going out on the water in the first place is the element of risk. We are all aware of it, and we know we aren't going to get out and walk if our boat leaves us, so we take every precaution to avoid a mishap. Personally, I feel safer in a boat than I do on a highway with a couple of tons of steel coming at me at 70 mph.

Besides the usual life preservers and cushions for all, there are a few items to toss into a boat to increase safety. A bailing dish is one of them, and oars, too, along with a spare oarlock. None of these items should be omitted. In some areas it would probably make sense to carry an anchor and rode, but here on the Maine coast, where I do my sailing, there is little chance of blowing to Europe from losing an oar or something, because there are plenty of weighted lobster traps handy with a line on them ready and available to tie to. I don't recommend grabbing onto one of these lines except in case of emergency, for to do so is to invite the wrath of a fisherman, who will perhaps have to spend hours tracking down his lobster pot after you have dragged it for a mile or two.

Lobster fishermen are observant, cautious, and cagey. They have to be because most of them work alone, and their lives depend on their wits. I thought I'd heard of about every means of survival in my lobstering career until just recently, when my brother-in-law and fellow lobster fisherman, Edgar Post of Spruce Head, said, "Did you know that rockweed makes a good life preserver in case you get stranded on a half-tide ledge and your boat has gone off and left you?" I hadn't thought of it, and probably few boatmen have.

Edgar never misses much that goes on around him, and while tending his herring weir one day, he noticed that the heavily weighted twine around his "pocket" (that's an enclosure for holding fish) had gone slack between the water level and the top rail, which the twine was attached to. The apparent reason for the slack twine was the accumulation of rock weed that had drifted into the pocket, clinging to the twine and lifting it. Deducing that if rockweed could lift that much weight, it also might work as a life preserver, Edgar tried it out—stuffing his shirt and trousers full of it. He found that it floated him like a cork stopper.

That's a nice thing to know, especially when you stop to think that most of us, upon falling overboard into a raft of the stuff, would probably push it aside and pick a nice clear place to drown.

LET THE WINDS BLOW

There are no provisions made for reefing the Instant Boats' spritsails. If you feel endangered by too much wind, or speed, and find yourself getting soaked when flying along—say, on a broad reach (that's roughly with the boat at right angles to the wind)—then bring the bow up closer to the wind and she will slow down, where you can jog along, staying dry by keeping just enough headway on her for steering.

If on a run (that's with the wind behind you) and your boat feels as if she's yawing too much (bow going from side to side and the boat hard to steer), turn her into the wind, unstep the mast, furl the sail, and stow the rig. Go home under oars.

I always think of going home as going downwind, because I make a habit of striking off to windward from my mooring, and do most of my sailing upwind until I'm ready to come home.

As the prevailing southwest breeze in my area is usually chilly, I find it a pleasure to make the last leg of the trip a downwind run, which gives me a chance to warm up and to enjoy the sensation of a quiet ride without any thrashing or taking spray aboard. When conditions are favorable and you're not overworked from steering, it seems you could sail on forever.

MORE ADVANTAGES OF LIGHT WEIGHT

The more you use your Instant Boat, the more you will be aware of the benefits of its lightness. Running into something is one of them, and when you find that only paint has been scraped off from running her over a rock or into a wharf, there is that big feeling of relief that nothing has cracked or you haven't "holed" her, as is often the case in heavier boats.

That none of the Instant Boats has pivoting leeboards has never bothered me, for again, when you run aground, their light weight saves you from being hung up for long or cracking anything. I've run the Zephyr onto a mussel bed or a ledge a number of times, and got her off again quickly by shifting my weight to the side away from the leeboard. That will usually do it; if not, I reach over and pull the leeboard up a little and off she goes.

Another advantage of light weight is the unlimited possibilities of exploring. I love to beachcomb and never hesitate to put the Zephyr right up on the beach if the pickings look promising. I just sail her in close, take the leeboard and rudder up at the last moment, and drive her right on, leaving the sail to flutter if there isn't much wind.

Quite often I overstay my visit, finding the urge to discover what is around the next corner too hard to resist. When that happens, it's nice to know that I can get the Zephyr down to the water and overboard again by myself, even though the tide has gone off and left me.

Yes, there are a lot of advantages to building and using one of these small Instant Boats, and this book has space to cover only a few of them. There are a lot of things to learn and do, but reading about them isn't going to produce a boat for your adventures. The best way to find out the pleasures in store is by your own experience, and that adventure begins when you build your first boat.

Index